T0121419

Being a Parent

Also by Neena Sawant

Parenthood: A Mirage Or An Oasis
In Indian languages
Eka Talyat Hoti (Marathi)
Chahul Tarunyachi(Marathi)
Tamhara Balakno Oolkhavo (Gujarati)

Being a Parent

An Experience to Remember

NEENA SAWANT

PARTRIDGE

A Penguin Random House Company

Copyright © 2014 by neena sawant.
Cover Design & Sketches: Gopi Kukde

ISBN: Softcover   978-1-4828-1585-6
               Ebook   978-1-4828-1584-9

All rights reserved. No part of this book may be used or reproduced by any
means, graphic, electronic, or mechanical, including photocopying, recording,
taping or by any information storage retrieval system without the written
permission of the publisher except in the case of brief quotations embodied in
critical articles and reviews.

Because of the dynamic nature of the Internet, any web addresses or links
contained in this book may have changed since publication and may no longer
be valid. The views expressed in this work are solely those of the author and
do not necessarily reflect the views of the publisher, and the publisher hereby
disclaims any responsibility for them.

To order additional copies of this book, contact
Partridge India
000 800 10062 62
www.partridgepublishing.com/india
orders.india@partridgepublishing.com

Contents

Sowing the seed

The Nurturing

Teen Times

This book is dedicated to my dearest mother for her tireless pursuit of excellence in parenting!

Some thoughts . . . .

Parenting was never easy and it has become even more difficult in today's era of competition, speed and insecurity. In India children are always considered as equivalent to God and if a son is born families rejoice as if Lord Krishna has taken birth in their house and if it is a girl she is considered to be Goddess Lakshmi. Hence the love and affection given to children is enough to spoil them. One therefore needs emotional and intellectual help whilst bringing them up. Values form an integral part of teaching in every Indian household due to the religious beliefs followed by all. Preparing for motherhood, inculcating value based education with discipline, communicating with children therefore has become an essential aspect of rearing children.

Children will always be playful and mischievous. It is for the parent to realize if there are behavioral or academic problems or whether the child is hyperactive or disobedient especially in the school going age. Adolescence is a phase of growing up where there are intense emotional and physical changes in a child's development process. Adolescence has often been mired with controversies due to the inability of parents and children to understand each other, with each alleging the other to be difficult. Though as parents we have been through the same phase of development, most of us just do not take into account the changing environment or the stimuli available which have an impact on the child's development.

This is all the more important because today the problems faced by parents are far more different than those faced by the previous generation. Most children of today find mobile phones a necessity than a need, so also with the need for pocket money, going to pubs, need to be accepted by a group and so on. The list seems endless because today the culture is changing at a very rapid pace and globalization has fulfilled the dreams of the common man. So who is at fault: the parent for providing or the child for demanding? If one looks at the scene then there is no right or wrong—it is just your perception of the situation.

In these changing times parents themselves are at a loss for trying to communicate with their child or trying to find the right words. It is therefore important that the parent of today is in the right frame of mind to understand the issues of peer pressure, career decisions, sex education, hormonal changes, unisex fashion, metro sexual males and cupid who strikes these youngsters probably every month. The parents of today were never prepared for this. Hence when a child wishes to be independent and feels it is his right to be so, it may be the parent who is at a loss, for the situation is entirely new to him.

As parents of today's children one must take into account the rapid pace of education and the changing societal structure. Most of us have been brought up in an environment where dad made all decisions and we followed them. Most of us were also in awe or scared of our parents to express our thoughts or emotions. This is not the scenario today, as you find even a 5 year old questioning you. In teen times, parents find it all the more difficult to answer questions and often take the easy way out by being the authoritarian parent and saying they know what is best for the child. Thus begins a multitude of problems.

In all fields of education there is a concept of continuing education with refresher courses being held to update a person in that field. I feel that the same should be made available to parents so as to provide insights into the development of the ever changing adolescent so that the parents are armed with the skills of communication, knowledge and understanding and handling of the children.

This book is an initial attempt to help parents identify the problem areas and understand dealing with their child. It is for us as parents to change to bring about the change we want in our child!

Neena Sawant
Mumbai, India
31ˢᵗ December, 2013

Sowing the seed . . . . .

This section is on the beginning of pregnancy and life, values imparted to children and the need to have family ties.

1 *The Beginning Of Life—To Be A Mother*

The most important thing in a woman's life is to be a mother. Her joy knows no bounds when she realizes she is expecting her first born, the ultimate pleasure being holding the bundle of joy close to her bosom. Every woman goes through the throes of when would she be a mother? Some are lucky i. e. they do not have to wait for long to fulfill their wish but in today's changing times many married couples don't immediately jump into parenthood post marriage.

What with working couples, sometimes making a family is a faraway dream. Today most women are career oriented or are seeing to it that they are at least financially independent. In this economic struggle, to be on one's own feet is at times a priority than starting a family. Also many couples feel that they should be in a position to give their child the best, hence the wait.

Today's changing times have caused a lot of change in peoples lifestyles. No longer are things just for the rich but a necessity for the common man. Eating out in restaurants, going for movies, weekend outings etc. have become practically a daily routine. Today people are not scared of spending because they feel they are earning enough and many generally just fend for themselves than look after the whole family. The nuclear family structure has also contributed to this change where now, in times of need, your own kin may think twice before giving monetary help.

Such changing values definitely have an impact on the psyche of the person. Also all this struggle has caused a lot of stress in the people. Most of the working class is handling the office and home front all by themselves and so they keep on juggling to keep the stress at bay. An average working woman gets up early, makes lunch packs of husband and kids and of anyone else at home, catches her train/bus and returns late evening. Where is the time to spend chatting with her husband or friends or just relaxing? Cooking is done with the T. V. on and so is the eating. Communication has drastically reduced and is only what is shown on T. V. Having sex may sometimes be cast aside in her mind because there are dishes to be done and the preparation for tomorrows cooking. In this entire jumbled world where and when will she think about a family?

This happens to be a major lifestyle change in women, as they are so preoccupied with chores that, they cannot think of a baby. People working as executives in MNC's have a different story to tell. They earn very well but their working hours progress beyond 12 hours of duty and may sometimes go beyond midnight. How are the women going to survive in this I. T. Industry? When these women get pregnant, a lot of problems emerge. Due to their hectic lifestyle many of them don't pay attention to their eating or physical fitness which is an essential thing in the first 3 months of pregnancy. As a result of this a lot of complications emerge—the fetus may not be developing properly and abortions happen frequently. Some of the abortions many be spontaneous i. e. the woman may have bleeding and she loses her baby or sometimes the baby has to be aborted because of medical problems.

Looking back at the previous generations, people did not have so many problems in conceiving, nor were the rates of abortion so high. Obviously the women were hardworking but they were also fit and looked after their health. Today's pregnant woman eats very cautiously because she does not want excess weight. Hence when healthy food gets compromised, so does the baby's health. Stress is one important factor which causes a lot of problems in sleeping, eating habits and general emotional well being. The expectant mother also may have emotional upheavals with sudden outbursts of crying, irritability, and sadness of mood. Many of them feel unhappy with the pregnancy status and in that negative frame of mind do think about abortion. Many may suffer from vomiting, nausea which is seen in the first trimester and find it difficult to cope with the physical symptoms.

Due to the hormonal changes occurring during pregnancy, depression and anxiety are commonly seen. As a result of this many women feel hopeless, feel the pregnancy is useless and that no one cares for them etc. Many of them complain of severe body aches and pains with giddiness and due to the pregnancy status, women also cannot take any medication without the doctor's advice. Hence, it becomes a very difficult state for the woman as she has to look after her physical self, home and job. Sometimes this takes its toll and results in the increasing number of abortions.

After the abortion a multiple range of emotions may emerge. If the woman was already feeling depressed early in the pregnancy she will feel more hopeless and useless. She will feel guilty and may blame herself and others for the loss. She may take time in getting to terms with her current condition, and she may lose all interest in life and surrounding. Many may also feel apprehensive and worried about future viz, if they would have a child, whether the child would be healthy, whether they would be blamed by in laws for the abortion etc. ? When the woman starts manifesting these symptoms which are present for more than 10 days then she should be started on medication to improve her emotional well being. If the symptoms are of a lesser intensity then the woman can be taken up for counseling sessions to help her cope with the loss. With due course of time, the scars heal and the woman can think of conceiving again only after 3 months when she is physically and emotionally stable.

Being emotionally stable is an important aspect of pregnancy because the emotions which the woman goes through are very strong and if she is persistently in a low mood, the fetus gets only negative vibes. Positive vibes are essential for the better bonding of the mother and child during the pregnancy state. Hence treatment of the mother at the earliest is essential. But the family does not realize this, and the woman may also not get adequate leave from her office to recuperate and so she is in a hurry to start work without the proper healing of the body and the mind.

Hence it is very important that when planning for a baby one has to do it at the right time (when the mother is physically fit) and with the right frame of mind (when there is a positive feel towards the child). The pregnancy will sustain, provided adequate care, proper exercise; sleeping and eating regimens are maintained. Late nights, drinks, junk food, excess coffee, alcohol or drugs (other medication) and all things which may have a bad impact on the fetus' health should be avoided.

Lastly, sometimes one may have to decide between career and family and if the career is coming in the way of starting a family i. e. increasing the stress, causing physical drain and disturbing the lifestyle then the woman should sit back, think and communicate with all her near and dear ones about continuing the job and then take a decision, for, in life to gain something you have to give up something. Hence the right decision will help the woman to achieve what she always wanted.

2 *Family Ties*

India as a country is very rich in its culture, diversity and most important of its attachment to the soil, to the people and to its families. Peep into any household and you will find the ties of attachment very strong. People talk with passion about their native places, homeland, forefathers and of course their families. India can proudly boast of its strength in unity but now because of increasing urbanization and modernization, there is a dramatic shift and migration of people to the urban cities in search of livelihood and no longer are people staying back in villages. They are venturing into the alluring cities which are beckoning them with enticing prospects. There is nothing wrong in this, as it is essential, that we progress as a nation.

But in the midst of all this, something has happened to the family structure. As the man walked out of the house in search of livelihood, the family was left behind the village. However the basic joint family structure was maintained as the women and children stayed together whereas the men left the village. The men would visit them a couple of times a year when they would spend about a couple of months with their family.

But now, even that picture is changing as many men who have got settled in cities would call for their wives and children to stay with them. So the joint family structure gave way to the nuclear family structure. Now majority of the families in cities are nuclear families or extended families with only the grandparents staying with the son and his family. No longer in cities will you see uncles, aunts, cousins staying under one roof. Another factor that is responsible is the lack of space and economic restraints which make it difficult for all the people to stay under one roof.

The concept today is to have a small family i. e. mother, father and one child or at the most 2 children. People are satisfied in having few children because there is lack of space and the cost of raising a child is very high in the city. Hence to be able to give the child a proper education and for his well being, there is a big move from the government, to prevent population explosion. All this has had an impact on the family's general and emotional wellbeing.

Today in the nuclear family, many times both the husband and wife are working to make ends meet. Hence both leave the house in the morning and come only late in the evening. The nuclear family with a working woman has a lot of impact on the emotional well being of the family members. Savita a 35 years old married woman was staying in Mumbai with her husband and son. Her husband worked as a peon and she was working in a garments factory. Savita had come to me with complaints of feeling fatigued, not able to do her household work, problem at concentrating and making mistakes at workplace and feelings of irritability and anger outbursts which she found difficult to cope. Initially her in-laws were staying with her and her mother-in-law helped her in looking after the house and taking care of her son. Now she had to do all the work alone. She did not have any time for herself and her husband often came home late, so there was no help from him either. Her son had also become very demanding and she was keeping him in a crèche. Her irritability increased beyond limits and she would thrash her son every day. Her husband had told her to leave the job but Savita knew that it was impossible to run the house. She was in a fix as her in-laws had separated due to the fights between her mother-in-law and her. She had now realized how much social support she had when they were staying with her. Due to this problem, she had suffered from depression.

This picture is seen in every household where there are extended families. There are a lot of interpersonal problems between the members as a result of which everybody takes the easy way out i. e. separation. This was not a picture seen before. Before the elders in the family would sit together and try to solve the issue and would try to see that the joint family structure remains. Today, people do not want to interfere and feel that every individual takes his own decision. This has worked against the benefits which a joint family structure provides i. e. sharing, caring, participating, supporting each other in times of financial crisis, illness, household work etc. There is a lot of emotional and financial security in the joint family households as people feel the joy and sorrow. Joint families help to build strong ties and bonds and a person learns to think and feel beyond himself or herself. A joint family system teaches individuals to work in a group which also helps in other spheres of life.

Sadly as the joint family structure is crumbling, a lot of families face helplessness as they are coping alone in illnesses, crises and everyday life situations. This also has resulted in a lot of emotional stress in individuals leading to anxiety, depression, physical illnesses, sleeplessness and other problems like alcoholism and behavior problems.

Major effect is seen on children in nuclear families with working mothers. Children are kept in day care and there is very little time that the child has with his parents. Also the child does not develop the attachment ties as he is often by himself. Children may also develop behavioral problems and they may become aggressive, irritable etc. Parents may not have enough time to take the studies which is often the responsibility of the tuition teacher. In the joint family there may be 2-3 kids of the same age who often study together or an elder child takes their studies. The child always has somebody to run to if he is hurt or he wants something. Children also have a lot of role models in the joint family to imbibe good qualities and they have enough friends in the house itself to play, so that they don't feel alone. They also learn to share their toys, clothes, books and eatables as a result of which they become responsible children.

An only child in a nuclear family is very possessive of his things and is often insecure about his emotions. Hence he will not easily share and would often be demanding, prone to throwing temper tantrums. Of course, with changing societal needs and the societal structure, families have also become extended, nuclear to single parent families. Man has to keep pace with these changes and so he has to prepare himself for it. Many families go through various adjustments problems when the family structure changes.

What people have to understand is that they have to communicate with each other to maintain the bonds of attachment. Coming home and sitting in front of the television is a common thing done today instead of talking about one's day at work with one's, spouse, children or parents.

Families of today have to do more in terms of emotional needs to maintain the sanctity in the relationships. There has to be allotment of work with sharing of duties to achieve normality in each household and to prevent any one member from suffering from the brunt of overwork. Whatever happens, nuclear family is a thing of today, so we should thrive to keep the family as intact as possible. Joint families will always be welcome as they are the foundation stone for any family.

Hence be it a joint or nuclear family, we should feel committed to the family structure and take responsibility as individuals of that family to handle the interpersonal, social or economic problems that may arise. If the individuals in a family feel for each other, then that family can weather any storm.

3 *Growing Up*

The most wonderful thing in life is childhood! It is full of learning new things with increased curiosity and enjoying every moment without any worries of tomorrow! The feelings of security, happiness and joy engulf the entire childhood whereas the negative emotions like worrying, insecurity, fear are miles away. And that is why all adults feel once in a while 'Oh! To be a child again'— but then though the picture looks rosy it is not so, and all children go through the stages of growing up experiencing a wide range of emotions as they go through the development process. Pain and pleasure is a constant companion to an adult or a child and it is the parent who has to understand the emotion and be there to give a hug to the child if he experiences either pain or pleasure.

As a child is developing he goes through the various stages of development which include—emotional, intellectual, behavioral and social phases of development. At every stage the child experiences new ideas and thoughts to which he has his emotions which then shape his behavior. The various stages of development are broadly divided into infancy (up to 12 months), toddler (12 to 24 months), preschooler and school going children.

Parents, though aware that the child will go through the stages at his own pace, often start worrying and seek the doctor's advice when they see other children developing faster. Actually during the developing phases, a child learns new things over a period of 6-8 months. Hence some children may learn within a month whereas another child may take

8 months. This does not mean that the child is slow for development. A doctor couple had got their 2 year old son to show me because he was not "speaking". On enquiry the child was saying "baba, aai, dada" etc. but was still not saying small sentences. Hence, his father, an ENT surgeon was worried. The child was unaware of the anxiety he had created in his parent's minds as he happily mumbled to self and played with the ball. Here his father was talking about doing investigations; his mother was comparing his growth to her niece who was singing tunes at 2 years and hence all the apprehension.

On asking them the age at which he developed his motor milestones like sitting, standing, walking etc. both replied that all his milestones were normal except for talking. Sometimes as parents we don't have any other option than waiting patiently. It is a known fact that girls talk early as compared to boys. We have to remember that nature takes its own course—we cannot will rains to come or the sun to set in early or the sun to shine less brightly. These things are not in our hands—so is the development process! We just have to strike a right balance between allowing the child to grow by self than keeping his daily progress on a progress card. This will hinder his progress as we may take away the opportunity from him to self-learn if he does not develop that milestone.

Hence I told the couple, to keep on talking to their child as they normally would, without stressing for a reply from the child or expecting the same from the child. The process is to let him understand the new words, learn them, associate them and then use them. Parents should let their child explore the world of language, as he/she learns to roll his/her tongue over the `r's and let him/her have fun saying it. Many parents try to butt in and tell the child "don't say like this but say it like that . . . ." What is the child going to understand? For him `pa' is father, grandfather as well as water. It is only later that he will differentiate the words and the meanings.

Children are like sponge. They pick up everything they see, hear or speak. They do not know the meaning of `importance' and so everything they learn or hear is "important" whether it is a phrase, a song or even verbal abuses. Hence they will say everything in the same breath. It is only the parent who feels embarrassed if the child uses bad language, because only the parent is aware of the meaning. Hence when explaining to the child, one has to understand his level of development and understanding to give the explanation. Therefore giving complex meanings makes no sense to the child who uses some words because he likes their sound, or he can roll the words or others get angry. Hence knowing his intellectual development, the parent would have to explain to him why that particulars word is banned from his dictionary.

As the child is growing up, he/she also has his/her own feelings to all that is around him. The most terrible thing a parent can do is to be unaware of their child's thoughts and emotions, like or dislikes about particular things, ideas etc. A child often expresses his feelings in behavior rather than saying it out aloud. He may not say he "enjoyed the ice-cream" but will definitely say "I want more ice-cream" to depict the same emotion. As children cannot express in words, parents often misconstrue that they do not have emotions. As a result of this they saddle their desires and wishes onto the children and every time the child refuses to comply with the parents wish, the child is then called stubborn or beaten up by the parent. But did the parent try to find out what the child felt about the task or did they find out why he didn't do it? This thus happens to be the common mistake that parents do—and the child gets labeled "as someone who doesn't listen" or "one who back answers" etc.

If we want our children to have good reasoning powers and be able to judge good from bad and to do well in life, it also means that we should spend more time when they are growing up. We should help them understand the changes in their mind and body and be physically and emotionally present for them when they express help. A secure attachment with parents and a supportive stimulating environment, all help the intellectual, emotional and behavioral growth of the little one.

Children very often are silent observers. Hence how we behave towards them or others reflects in their behavior with friends and family. For children usually the role models are parents and teachers. Their beliefs are firmly laid down "Mummy is always right," "My teacher is always right". Hence they often behave accordingly. Also they keep the 2 areas—school and home separate. Hence the teacher's rule is followed at school and mom's at home. If mom tries to tell something else about the homework, it is suddenly vetoed for "my teacher has said this is to be done only in this way . . . ." The parent has to understand that the child behaves so because, he has still not learnt the ability to abstract which is a higher level of thinking which develops around 11-12 years of age. The child at that age can imagine the consequences and can come to his own conclusions and will formulate his own strategies to solve problems. Hence parents should not expect this from a young child.

The problem with all parents is that, though, they know that the child is small they expect the child to behave and understand things like the adult. Children will have to be told things time and again with proper reasons like for e. g., if the parent says "Don't jump on the sofa or else the sofa springs will break and then you will not be comfortable sitting on the sofa when watching your favorite T. V. program" will probably make the child understand more what his mother wants than just saying "Don't jump". Children are curious by nature and have lots of questions in their minds but since childhood the home atmosphere is such that, in many households questions are not welcome. Hence many a question remains unanswered and the child loses the opportunity to express his thoughts and feelings.

It is very important to make the child feel that he can opine and his opinion is considered valid. When doing my children's room I asked my 9 year old daughter to select the bathroom tiles. Obviously the little girl was awed by the sight of so many varieties and could not understand. Gradually zeroing down to 2-3 samples I quietly pointed out the color schemes and she made her choice. Of course I had phrased my questions and answers to make her and my approval coincide so as to make her selection easy. But she feet really proud of her decision and went on telling everybody that she had chosen her tiles. Many a times we take the decisions for our children. In important issues it is mandatory, but more often it is the parent v/s child's decision. Let there be discussion in the house even if it is on mundane day to day activities like which studies should we do today, what should mamma prepare tonight or which T. V. program to watch?

After all, every parent wants his or her child to reach the stars and that would happen only if we stimulate our child's thinking process, make him or her aware of his emotions and inform them about their behavior. Ultimately as a gardener tends to his garden, all parents have to look after to their children, tending to their needs, giving love and affection and then see them bloom like the flowers. Though, it is not difficult it is not easy either. After all parenting is a task and requires a prefect balancing of the parental expectations and the child's desires. But as parents, it is necessary that we do not forget that the little ones have a mind of their own which we have to nurture!

4 *Telling Children About Values*

India is a diverse culture which is embedded with long standing traditions and cultural values. Every religion has its beliefs which are followed by the people of that religion. So rich is the culture, that India is looked upon a place where people of diverse cultures stay together in harmony. These traditions are all the moral values that have been taught to each and every individual which is called "Sanskar"(values).

Actually values do not have to be taught for more often they are learnt by watching others. For e. g. if we teach children that one should always tell the truth or one should be honest and one should own up if one has done wrong then as parents we should be following the same. The child gets mixed messages if we do the opposite but continuously tell him what is right or wrong. Some children may also question their parents about the same, but parents put them off by saying that "don't back answer", "you are too young to understand" or "we are your parents, so we know what's best".

A child starts believing in those values if he sees it happening in his house everyday as a routine. For e. g. a child starts believing in God and develops religious beliefs because he finds his parents, his grandparents praying. He sees them doing it every day, he hears the prayers, he's told the meaning of the prayers and so he inculcates this belief. Hence, he does not offer prayers only when he has exams or when he desires something but offers prayers every day for general wellbeing. Believing in something, helps to develop trust, makes one feel secure and gives a feeling of oneness with society.

The environment in which the child is brought up is therefore important. It is necessary for parents first to realize their ideals and then go towards achieving them. Talking nicely to members of the family, enquiring about their needs, respecting elders builds the platform for making social relationship stronger. The child learns by seeing every day. Hence the language he will use with others will also have that tone. Parents are scared to send children down to play because they will learn "bad words". But if they themselves abuse as many of us do it in a fit of anger, it is not friends but us from whom the child learns. Instead of beating the child for abusing, the parent should tell him the meaning of the word and then ask the child how he would feel it someone told him the same. It is then re-inforced on the child that the other person feels very hurt because of saying such things. Giving the same message to the child makes him realize and he stops using bad words.

A parent once told me that his child uses the word 'bastard' for everyone including the parents when angry. They would often beat the child but to no avail. I asked the parents if they had discussed the meaning of the word with their child and they looked at me horrifically. I then spoke to their child who said that everyone in his class called each other "bastard". I then very simply explained the meaning to him and asked him if he would like to be called a bastard? He said, "no" and then I told him that since his friends had their parents with them, so calling them bastards was foolish and he definitely was not foolish. His frequency of using the bad word came down but I am sure he would have caught on another one. What is therefore important is a little bit of communication to solve matters.

More often, it is how we communicate, how strongly we believe in things that actually sets up these traditional values. Of course with changing trends in society, most of the families have given up on many traditions and hence children are not exposed at all to any of the value systems. Such are the trends that telling lies, trying to fool people to have your way has become a way of life for many people and this is what the young children are continuously exposed to. Help your neighbor, keep your surroundings clean are now a thing of the past. The surrounding is very much limited to one's house and hence children have no civic sense as they litter everywhere in schools, roads, gardens etc. but if an alert parent or a passerby reprimands them and picks up the litter and throws it in the bin, children would feel ashamed and would definitely think twice before littering.

One does not have to discipline children to make them follow traditions. For e. g. teaching a child that he has to keep himself clean to remain healthy by giving examples, by doing it oneself will make the child realize that brushing and taking bath twice daily, washing hands etc. is essential rather than the parent reminding him to do it every day.

Every parent actually wants their child to be a good human being. One cannot imbibe only good values, one also has some negative values. What is essential is that a child learns to differentiate between what is, right or wrong. Parents should also realize that with changing trends value systems also change. Hence they should be more open in accepting the change and allow the children to experience and experiment. They should themselves also experience and experiment. If there is communication between the parent and the child, the parent has to be authoritarian than being autocratic or a dictator. He should take into consideration the child's view point, should put forth his own views and fears especially if the children are adolescents and are getting influenced by media, fashion etc. before degrading any culture or putting it across to them that "we never did it in our time," "this is vulgar" etc.

Children are open to suggestions and it depends on how you talk to them. When they are adolescents they want to break rules, be independent and have their own way. That is the time when there is intense turmoil and a lot of backlash on values and traditions by the children. One has to understand that parenting is a difficult job and during the phase of adolescence it is a very trying experience. But if one believes one ideals and one has been following them, then the children also get influenced by them. They may just need a little guidance when they are faced with changing values, but if the parent is concerned and considerate all that value education does not go waste. Somewhere it touches the chord in the child who then respects the age old traditions. The old and the new traditional systems do merge to make way for the changing value systems but in the end they do question the integrity of the values.

Let us ourselves inculcate values and they will definitely be imbibed by our children! Some ideas to help you:

Tell your own examples and stories

Kids love to hear stories about your childhood. Tell about some good and bad incidents by weaving in some moral dilemmas. Children learn more from such stories than a monotonous lecture.

Be a good role model

Kids learn by imitating, especially at a young age. They are very adept at seeing if what you say and what you do are matching up. Don't give them confusing signals; follow your own values every moment.

Teach them your religion or faith

Your children should be aware of the religion or faith followed in the house. Meeting other people doing the same or taking them along for religious functions will strengthen their values. Tell them stories and the importance of faith. Today times are changing and so is the belief in religious faith. Inculcating this would help to restore faith and trust in each other.

Know others who will teach them values

Get to know your child's teachers, coaches, relatives, etc. Anyone who spends time with your kids may be influencing them. Know their values and beliefs as well, especially the maids who looks after them.

Make them think and question about values

Just telling them what values they should have won't always be effective, especially when your kids get older. Asking them "pertinent" questions will allow discussions that will eventually lead to values. "What did you think about that fight? Who is wrong?" may be more effective than, "He shouldn't have started that fight!"

Do not preach

There's nothing that will turn your kids off more than preaching values to them after they've made mistakes! Talk to them when everyone's relaxed without reprimanding them in front of all but listening to their point of view before giving your own.

Cultivate helping habits

Kids learn values when they experience them. Allow them to experience helping others and involve them in activities that will expand their creativity.

Talk about values in your household

This lets your kids know that values are important and it's not just something you talk about when they do something wrong. Praise them for their good deeds by quoting their example to your friends and relatives. It is your way of appreciating their efforts and of course reinforcing the behavior.

Finally let us try to be good human beings and for sure, our children will follow!

5 *Character Development*

"A man is known by the company he keeps"—is something which we are all familiar with and believe in. What it actually talks about is our temperament and attitudes as a result of which we get along with likeminded individuals. All of us have our own distinctive personality, as a result of which we respond to life situations differently. For example, if 3 people were stuck in a lift, each might react differently. One might crack jokes to relieve the tension, one may be very tense and anxious and may make predictions that "we would never get out of here" whereas the third may be calm and may think about ways to escape. These varied reactions to the same situation occur because each person has a different personality. Each person has traits that are seen in other people, but each individual has his or her own distinctive set of personality traits.

It is easy to say that 'Ami is shy' or 'Sharad is aggressive' which in fact are a part of one's personality and when we talk about a person's attitudes and aptitudes we are actually referring to personality traits like moody, honest, dependable, impulsive, anxious, suspicious, excitable, domineering, friendly etc. There are more than 4500 personality traits identified and individuals may have several such traits but each of us may have certain cardinal traits which characterize nearly all of person's behaviors like the need to do things for others as seen in Mother Teresa or aggression and dominance as seen in Hitler.

We may be able to identify such cardinal or central traits in individuals by means of which we form opinions like:

- Sheetal is an anxious, insecure, guilt prone and self-conscious girl (which indicates "neuroticism")
- Jai is a talkative, lovable, fun loving and affectionate boy (which indicates "extraversion")
- Amit is daring, nonconforming, shows broad interests and is creative and imaginative (which means "openness to experience")
- Sucheta is a sympathetic, warm, trusting and cooperative girl (which indicates "agreeableness")

Our personality develops as we are growing up in our childhood and it usually gets formed by adolescence. A lot of factors are important in shaping our personality. It depends on the way we interact with people, with the environment and the reactions and responses on our mind. Hence when we talk about instilling moral and cultural values on children, it all has an impact on the cardinal personality traits.

It is also important how the people around us i. e. parents, peers, teachers etc, act as role models. For e.g. if a mother is a worrier, who is always anxious for the child's well being and keeps on protecting the child from any harm befalling on him/her—she may make him/her to be an anxious person when he/she grows up, due to faulty role modeling. Such a child may then be insecure of his/her own capabilities or may be dependent on others for decision making. He/she would remain anxious and unsure of himself/herself. Hence the right attitude with appropriate parenting skills would help in the development of positive traits.

Once one's "nature" (personality) is formed it becomes difficult to change it, because these traits then become "cardinal" to our living. What we always do as individuals is try to adapt our traits to suit the environment or people with whom we are continuously interacting. For e. g. as a daughter of the house, the girl would "tolerate" her mother's anxiousness and interference because of the fact that she is her 'mother' and so she cares for her but the same girl finds it 'difficult to tolerate' her mother-in-laws behavior which more or less would be the same as her mother's but as she does not accept the mother-in-law as a person who would care for her, she does not accept her ideals. All these clashes which go on in every family are actually the differences in the nature or 'personality' of the individuals involved and more so the ability of the mind to accept certain situations as "reasonable" and others as "unreasonable".

It is often spoken by people that so and so person is an extremely aggressive and violent person with a horrible temper at home but the same person is a very calm, cool and collected person at office. This happens to most of us and hence we should be aware that there are many shades to our personality and we do behave badly in certain situations depending on our pre-conceived notions, ideas, beliefs, our expectations and the environment. Many of us accept our faults by saying that "I am like that, you should not aggravate me" or "you bring out the worst in me" but then we do nothing to change ourselves or correct our wrong notions. This lassitude on our part to bring out the best in us is responsible for the same reactions that keep on occurring when faced with the same situation. Hence a pattern of responses to certain reactions are formed and we get into the world of "Daughter in law—Mother in law", "Boss-Employee", "Mother-Child", "Friend-Friend" etc. kind of behaviors. An era of such response makes us believe in these responses even if they are wrong or not suitable for us but because "this has been the way . . . . I have always behaved" or "I am like this only" and we refuse to do otherwise.

Hence, it is difficult to expect anyone above 30-35 years to listen to somebody younger or see another person's "point of view". Stubbornness is therefore a trait in all adults in their middle ages and a complaint of the younger generation. After a particular age it becomes difficult for people to change their ways of thinking, the emotions attached to those thoughts and the behaviors that ensue as a result. At such an age when we become parents things become all the more difficult. Our child will always find this "generation gap" though you may be only 20 years older to him. As parents we find it difficult to acknowledge that things are changing and because our parents behaved strictly with us we become unreasonable and do the same with our young ones.

Hence adaptability is a feature seen in the younger generation who when growing up always adjust to the temperament and environment. Hence a young person getting selected to a job requiring shift duties will have problems initially but gets adjusted to the sleep-wake patterns in a minimum time contrary to an older man who has tremendous difficulty when faced with the situation for the first time.

Being exposed to various environments also teaches people different ways of coping with situations which eventually also shapes our personality. Hence for every individual to develop to his or her fullest potential it is essential that one uses one's intellectual prowess coupled with one's emotional resources to tide over the situation. Children who are given opportunity to experiment and learn from experimentation, have a different outlook and perspective than a child who has been always told to do things in a particular way and not allowed to develop. Ultimately all this is what makes a person reserved or outgoing or stubborn or indecisive. These qualities get ingrained in us as we are developing and hence as we imbibe them, we should also allow our thoughts to change, so that the behavior changes. A positive outlook with the thought that "Yes I can do it" will go a long way in making us self-dependent, resilient individuals. A change in making is a change for the better, as we try to break the orthodox conservative moulds to learn from newer technologies and perspectives in this ever changing environment. It is ultimately in our hands to reach for the stars and it is equally important to do a self-appraisal so that we are aware of our positive and negative sides.

Positive thinking, setting goals, getting started, reasoning, problem solving, listening and doing are some of the things which help us to develop emotionally and intellectually. Channelizing our creativity and talent will bring out the best in us which will eventually boost our morale and self-esteem and will change our perception of looking at things.

Doing yoga, meditation to relax the mind or de-stress oneself, helps in clearing the cobwebs and a calm mind is in a better frame to think rationally. All this would help us in our day to day dealings which then has an impact on us as an individual. Feeling good, being good and doing good gives an immense sense of satisfaction and does wonders for our self-esteem. There are always 2 sides to a coin so also there are always 2 points of view.

Let us make an attempt to understand the other side, before deciding that it should always be done this way. Understanding, then deciding will help us in problem solving which is the need of the day. Let us as individuals make ourselves more open, more approachable and accessible for change than being orthodox in our views and this would be a great state to developing ourselves into ideal people or personalities.

Ultimately our temperaments are equally important in shaping our kids personalities.

The Nurturing....

This section is on importance of disciplining, importance of communication with children, the common problems seen in 5-10 year olds—admission to schools, not listening, TV watching, behavior problems, hyperactivity, not studying etc

6 *Children & Discipline*

One day I was just discussing with my friends on the issue of disciplining children, and they turned about and told me "Neena, let's see how you are going to handle your children?" Your children probably are now listening to you because they are young but just wait till they become a little big, they, just don't listen! They back answer, don't bother to reply and at times behave such that we as parents feel as if they don't care for us ! Well I do agree with all parents who are going through the throes of parenting. "Discipline" is one major issue in many households.

None of us have ever gone to parenting schools to learn the 'Do's' and 'Don'ts'of parenting. Hence all of us practice parenting as per our own personal experience. We may have grown in an environment of discipline and hence as a parent we mete out the same to our child. If you look at mankind and its development you will find that for mankind to progress, it was very necessary to have social rules and regulations. Man obeyed these rules, followed them and hence has been able to achieve what he is today! If an early man living in caves could follow the rules to maintain peace and harmony, I think so can man living in the city.

What is discipline? Basically maintaining order, which is what we try to do in all spheres of our life. But when we are disciplining, we should also use our minds to think if that is what one wants to achieve in that situation. Today, man has become a blind follower of many rules which could be obsolete in today's world but he still follows them because 'a rule is a rule'! He does not verify with himself whether there really is a need to obey that rule. The result being that he lives with the rule and applies it in his workplace and at home. But just because he doesn't question the rules significance, doesn't mean that the other person won't. And when somebody opposes, there is a clash of interests and a conflict arises.

This is what is happening in parenting. Parents have been so much under the influence of the various regulations they grew up with and the cultural atmosphere where "you respect elders and take their opinion because they know all" and a tendency in the Indian culture where a young child could never meet his parent's eye and talk comfortably because he was too scared to ask. My parents used to proudly tell me that, "our father was strict, he made all the decisions and we followed them." Their era was such that most parents were "authoritarians" i. e. they dictated and children followed. We have seen too many films depicting the same themes and glorifying "discipline". Parents would feel extremely happy that their children were under their thumbs. But is this what we as parents want? I am sure some of us may have enjoyed our childhood without feeling the remorse when we gave into our parents' wishes after several thoughtful deliberations. Ideally rules make life easier—because it is like solving a problem. But when rules start becoming a problem—then one has to question the validity of that rule.

Parents should be authoritative i. e. firm but amenable to suggestions but not authoritarians i. e. `dictators". They should also not be very lax i. e. giving all the freedom and independence to the child to do what he or she wants—because children are not aware of the various pitfalls of the various decisions that they may take and hence it is essential that a parent talks over the things with them to make them realize and understand. The duty of the parent is to give his child independence in thinking—let him think of the situations, what can happen, what won't happen, are there options, what will work out best etc? Let your children think of the impossible, let them dream, hope and aspire! Let them challenge your beliefs—because from those will arise new answers and new beliefs!

Allowing children to challenge your beliefs does not mean that a child will not respect your decisions or you. In fact he will come closer to you because you as a parent understand him and are giving him an option of understanding you. As a parent one always wants to do the best for one's child—be it in education, providing amenities and life style. Give a child what he needs if only you feel the demand is reasonable. But don't give a child that for which he has no need or he doesn't understand its importance or value, or because you feel you have the money to buy the things which you feel he deserves. Love him—don't pamper him because if you pamper him—eventually he will "emotionally blackmail" you by throwing tantrums. And at that time all your disciplining goes out of the window. Because no parent is strong enough to handle the 'tantrums'— and yes then there is no point in hitting the child to show your inadequacy as a parent and the failure of all your rules and regulations.

Every parent should remember that if they lay the rules for children then they should lay down rules for themselves too. Parents should also follow the rules which then become applicable to the whole household so that the conflicts may not arise. Some rules will be meant only for children but then at times parents can be a little lax and forgiving rather than punishing the child. Like for e. g. if parents have said the child can play for an hour and the child plays for extra time, then the parent gets angry as the homework is not done.

This will be the story everyday—so to make matters easy, parents don't send the child down to play till he finishes his homework. But then here, the parent in behaving like a dictator and showing his ruler ship that he is a parent and so can command. But then this is not the answer to the problem. So the best way a parent can judge is by the amount of homework given, acknowledging the fact that the child has to finish it first, giving him a time limit for play for that particular day. The best thing is to consider 15 minutes extra play time in advance (in your mind), then to tell him that he could play for 45 minutes so when he comes up after 1 hour—that time was already calculated for.

Discussing with the child, also allows freedom of expression of the child and gives him the independence of taking his own decisions, which is actually what every parent wants. So then let us inculcate this habit in them when they are young, because if you have a responsible child, inevitably you have a disciplined child. If the parent only decides everything for the child—then there is an external discipline but no internal discipline, the thoughts and emotions have to come from within to be followed and then there is no need for the parent to be a tyrant and no need to say "Should I take the stick?"

Children are like clay, mould them to make better adults, to take different shapes—to have beautiful thinking and emotions, don't make them beautiful showpieces—for then they would remain in only one place and gather dust. Don't discipline them for improving their ability to express verbally, but to understand their thoughts and feeling and they will always respect you for that! Be there to stand by their side, not to admonish them but to cherish them! Be there to hold their hands, not to leave them unattended, be there to guide and they will take your guidance, discuss rules with them and they will follow you!

7 *Do We Talk To Our Child?*

Communication is an important aspect of one's life. How you communicate has an intense effect on what you communicate! Today, majority of the people communicate by emails, SMS's, letters etc. and very few actually have the time to talk to their heart's content. Such is the communication pattern all over the world that as parents we also do not have time to talk to our child and even if we do have, our speech is a very formal structured short sentence which hardly communicates our feelings and rarely creates that special bond. How was school? What did you eat? Have you any homework today? Go to your class! Clean your mess . . . . These are the words heard in every household. What happens then is that the children who actually have lots to say and discuss get confused and just answer what they have been asked. The rest is buried deep in their hearts and they also learn the language of "being short and sweet".

So where is the communication? To communicate means to share feelings, emotions and understand them. What is happening is that information is given but there is no sharing of the emotions associated with it. Hence a lack of bond between the parent and the child and the parent and parent then affects the relationship and many times we often try to blame others without realizing that somewhere the fault was within us.

In every household communication patterns differ as per the situation and the people involved. It is very important that when children are present, the right pattern of communication should ensue for e.g. many times the mother and father fight in front of children and children are exposed to facts and words they should not know. Parents forget that children are like sponges and they absorb all that is happening around them. Also children may use the information they receive to their advantage. Many a times the elders in the family also use children to relay information about others to them. For e. g. a grandmother may take her grandchild on her lap and then ask him "so what has your mother been saying about me" and the poor child who is innocent and unaware of the communication dynamics may blurt out to the grandmother the reality bites. Of course adults involve children in these games of theirs and then create a problem for a healthy relationship with the child.

The continuous bickering a common feature in most households may take an ugly turn when parental verbal abuses become physical fights which are then witnessed by the children. Many children feel helpless at that time because they love both their parents and cannot bear to see them fight. Many children may at times side with the mother and try to protect her from the father's fury thus turning the wrath on to them. It is a hopeless and helpless situation for any child to witness. A child who is nurtured in such an environment often feels insecure and experiences a lot of anxiety. Many children take cover behind the mother or under the sofa when the fights start. These children may then develop anxiety where they are restless, scared and worry about a lot of things. Their studies may also be affected because of the parental fights where they cannot concentrate and also get disinterested in studies. If the parents are not on speaking terms or there is some kind of a cold war going on at home, then the child often feels scared to leave the mother and fears that something may happen to her. Children then become overprotective and over concerned about their mother as they feel that the father may do something to her. More often than not, these anxieties are not expressed and the child keeps all these thoughts to himself or herself.

Parents may not even to aware that the child is going through so much of emotional trauma. Children may develop a variety of psychiatric manifestations due to the parental discord and the negative communication that happens between the parents. Older children, who can understand the situation but not the dynamics of marriage, helplessly wonder why their parents can't be like others and talk or joke properly.

These children can be prone for sleep disturbances, nightmares, depression and some children may be so tired of the daily fights that they even attempt suicide. Children may grow up feeling that nobody loves them and they have to look after themselves. Sometimes children will role model on these aspects of communication and may behave accordingly with their peers and seniors alike.

So then how do we combat all this? How do we make the environment conducive for the proper development of the child? Well as parents there are a few things that we have to learn.

1] Never fight in presence of others
2] When making your point, do not bring all other incidents into picture which is not relevant to the current issue
3] Try to be more expressive when communicating
4] Ensure that there is an equal share of positive as well as negative communication
5] Learn to say things tactfully
6] Listen to someone else's point of view.

Hence if a small change is brought in the way we look at things and we implement these changes, it will go a long way in helping parents to understand children and vice versa. Learn to praise each other as spouses rather than only pointing out to the faults. Communicating good things brings about good results. A child will then also learn the importance of things and the subject of moral science would not have to be taught if we actually practice morality and have a basic respect for the members of our household.

Discussing, explaining, listening, elaborating and understanding are the positive sides to any effective and useful communication. Ingraining these values will not only help the child in the long run but will also give you the pleasure of a satisfying relationship.

8 *It's Admission Time Folks*

Come January & February and a change is seen in all households, especially if there is a tiny tot getting ready to go to school. A lot of schools in India get ready for the preprimary admissions during this time. But what a nightmarish experience it is for the young one who still has to learn his A's, B's and C's. Schools have become notorious in keeping interviews for preprimary sections in order to select the best children for their school. These interviews are akin to 'high level exams' as it is the parents examination than their child's so all the playschools and parents alike start training the tiny tots on how to say their names, recognize shapes, colors, say poetry and probably a song and dance thrown in the bargain for the child to excel.

The poor child of course learns everything by rote memory without probably caring or understanding and then at the most needed moment in the principal's chamber refuses to say everything that has been taught. Getting a déjà vu? Well, it happens to all of us at one time or the other and I'm sure all parents would agree that it's the most harrowing experience. Imagine, if this is what a school interview does to us, then the effect on the children must be horrific. The only difference, is that we can vent it out by abusing the school, the government and even by beating the child if he had kept mum . . . . but what about the child ? Which one of us as parents asks our 3 or 4 year old, how it was to be in a new environment, with a stranger asking strange questions and NOT BEING SCARED?

The poor child is just bombarded day in and day out with questions and answers and told that he would be going for an interview but he may be completely unaware of the consequences. Is it his fault, that he may be interested in something else than the principal's question? Or he may not like the demeanor of that principal or he may be extremely scared of the new environment and may burst into tears. Even the tears don't move us as we continue to reprimand the child to show the results of our teaching than making him comfortable and holding him to our bosom. I have seen mothers hit out and berate their children in "this hour of need". We let our frustrations catch up on us and instead of fighting with the system; we fight with our children instead.

It is highly unethical for a school which is the foundation of education to be orthodox. Schools can observe children through play than formal interviews thus giving a breather to the parents if they want 'intelligent children'. It is definitely unconstitutional to select one over the other as children have the capacity to grow and will be molded by the teacher and parents alike. Hence every child has a right to education to the best school. This would call for government reforms and parents to unite against this emotional torture meted out to the children.

A child's performance depends on his dependency needs. If as parents we look after his emotional, mental and physical well being the child would definitely do well. So when admission forms are out and interview dates come, don't go on bombarding the child with new information which does not make sense, but give him a hug, a peck or two on his cheeks, ruffle his hair, take him on your lap, smile and then tell him that the Indian flag has 3 colors. Remember to praise him, cuddle him for the right answers and most important don't criticize him if he 'fails the interview'. IT IS NOT HIS FAULT, but yours for not fighting the wrong in the current educational system.

9 *TV Time*

"Mamma, what is cocaine? Why did he kill that person? Why are they dancing like that? Yuck . . . . They are kissing on T. V. !" These are the general expressions of a young school going child who is suddenly exposed to a variety of things happening around the world when the T. V. is on. The child who is continuously learning from the environment now learns new words, new actions and gives new meaning to different situation. And as parents we just helplessly look on . . . . Surfing the channels reveals the same scenes and the same information time and again thus giving a lot of importance to the situation. Children thus get exposed to unwanted and unwarranted stuff which may not be age appropriate when they sit in front of the T. V. And then comes the question "How much of the news or information should be seen or heard by children who may be of different ages and yet see the same stuff?"

This question has to be answered by every parent, for in today's era of e-communication and intense competition, every small news item gets a lot of media coverage with things being discussed at a great length on all T. V. channels. Even if the children don't want to see it they still do whilst flipping through the channels and unknowingly it leaves behind an imprint on their gullible minds.

There is a big hue and cry about how news channels show things that should not be shown and how on the basis of right to information, all kinds of news are allowed to be broadcasted. People also feel that news should be censored so that personal details are not made public. But for all this to change, one may have to wait. One also is unsure whether the news will become more blatant in future. Till then, parents will have to bear the impact this will have on the fragile minds of their children.

Parents are already preoccupied with the fact that their children are watching too much T. V. today with digital network displaying every possible channel in the world and with working parents, it has been difficult to control what a child watches on T. V. ! Seeing T. V. is not bad for a whole range of information is made available at the click of a button. There is a variety of educational information on national geographic, animal planet, pogo etc. with a whole lot of entertainment. Children are fond of cartoons, game shows, art and craft, movies and also animals.

But parents cannot expect children to see only educational films. They forget that children also require to laugh out, to enjoy themselves and break away from the routine of studies, studies and studies. There is also stimulation of the brain taking place when one is watching T. V. which is necessary for new learning. Hence, one should allow children to watch T. V. The next question that comes to parents' minds is how much T. V. should be allowed? Ideally an hour to one and a half hours is enough for the mind to concentrate, understand and enjoy after which the stimulation decreases and children or adults get distracted or bored of the same program. But parents should also watch the programs with their children so that they can monitor what their children are seeing. In order to bring discipline about TV time it may happen that all the members of the family would have to cooperate in giving up their TV time to model right behavior for the child. Hence mothers would have to give up some serials, fathers their news, grandparents their matches and movies for the little ones.

Sometimes a lot of aggression is shown in the various programs for children like power rangers, which the children may imitate and use in their everyday play. This may become dangerous as young children do not understand the implications when they start enacting what they have seen. There have been several reports of children copying stunts or doing aggressive scenes with repercussions. It also reflects that being aggressive is alright as all channels depict the same stories and children get used to hearing and seeing all these things day in and day out.

Hence, as parents one would have to curtail what the child watches by either putting a child lock on the various channels or being present in person to check the child's likes or dislikes. It also is mandatory for parents when questions are being raised by their kids to give some explanation so as to douse the child's curiosity rather than just look away or give some stupid answers. This usually happens when there are some sexual exploits, kissing scenes shown on T. V. and the child may have curiosity as regards to what the people are doing or advertisements regarding sanitary napkins when parents shy away from telling the truth or facts and just tell children 'that is dirty, it is not meant for you' etc. The child because, his questions are unanswered always has those thoughts at the back of his mind which he /she may then be blurt out in front of other people causing embarrassment to the parents.

As parents one has to remember that a lot of importance should not be given to the television in the house. Most households may have the T. V. set on even if no one is watching it. The time duration for the child to see his favorite program should be fixed and he should be allowed to see it. Rest of the time, the T. V. should be off. If possible it should be kept under lock and key in a cabinet or today the card should be removed from the set top box, without which there is nothing seen. Parents should spend some time with the children in telling bed time stories than exposing them to bed time serials. It may require a sacrifice of one or two serials on part of the mother till the child goes to sleep and the mother should see T. V. after the child is asleep.

To gain something, we have to lose something and so is the case with T. V. watching. Let the television not rule your household by deciding when the dinner time, study time or sleeping time should be, as is happening in many households for things are being changed to accommodate the various serials. The television is there for entertainment and it should remain like that only, for if your life as a parent revolves around it, it would not be long for your child to be completely besotted with the telly.

10 *Disruptive Kids*

Truly speaking behavior is not a constant phenomenon. It changes as per the situation and the environment. It depends on an individual's temperament which often shapes the behavior. Many times we have specific patterns of behavior when faced with certain situations. These usually develop and get re-enforced during our development phase and then becomes an integral aspect of our personality.

Children are highly notorious when they are being evaluated for behavior problems because many times parents are in a dilemma about whether it is normal behavior or there is a problem in their child. The child therefore may often go undiagnosed and untreated even if he is having a problem. There are several behavioral disturbances which may arise in children. The most common ones are hyperactivity, attention deficit, impulsivity, conduct disorder, oppositional defiant disorder and behavioral problems associated with mental retardation.

Varun was a nine year old boy who was brought by parents for constant lying and stealing. There were complaints from school regarding Varun's behavior. In class he would often hit other children, at times had torn books, he would snatch lunch boxes or throw pencils of others out of the window. He had turned abusive and his aggression was also mounting. At home he would pinch and hit his younger brother and would feel no remorse when his mother would shout or slap him. His parents had physically abused him many times as it was very difficult for them to control their anger, but they found no change in his behavior. He had also started stealing coins from his mother's purse which had got the mother worried. Varun's parents had thought that he was just a little aggressive than the other children and felt that he would improve on growing up. According to them he was very well looked after and all his demands were given into. Still they could not understand why he was behaving in this way.

Unfortunately his parents did not realize that Varun was in fact having a psychiatric problem called "Conduct Disorder". This disorder commonly presents in boys at 5 years of age and above and the behavioral problems are the most disturbing. These children are usually abusive, aggressive, vindictive, and have no remorse for their acts. They are also cruel to animals, may indulge in setting fire, running from home or school and they often steal and lie. Parents should be alert when these symptoms are present rather than just considering them as a part of growing up. These symptoms should be attended to and the child should be taken to the psychiatrist for assessment. If the behavior is very aggressive then low dose "antipsychotic" medication helps such children and the behavior comes under control. Talking to parents, educating them that this is an illness and that the child is not doing it deliberately is important to prevent child abuse. Beating the child will definitely not help in any way.

However, using behavior modification techniques will help in improving "wanted" or good behaviors. The parents are taught to give an incentive (which could be making the child's favorite dish, taking him out, giving him small prizes etc.) which will act as a reward or positive re-enforcement for the behavior which is wanted. Hence if the child does not steal / lie / abuse etc. the parent praises the child for his "good behavior" and gives the incentive. The parent should maintain a diary of the good behaviors done by the child and only if the behavioral change is persistent i. e. over 3 days, 5 days etc. then only the reward should be given.

Once the child understands this, he will try to change his behavior in order to get the reward. Parents also have to communicate with the child in order to know what's going on in his mind. Sometimes there may be fears which can be alleviated just by talking to the child. Usually it is seen that the child may lie about his failures, so if the parent talks to him, boosts his morale, finds out the child's strengths and weaknesses and tries to find a solution for the problem, the child may not have to lie at all.

11 *My Kids Are Not Listening*

We just understood about certain disorders which are major behavioral disorders in children. Sometime the child may not manifest a disorder but may have symptoms of anger out bursts, screaming, crying for attention etc. which are a common occurrence during the child's growing up phase. One such common problem encountered in children by parents is "temper tantrums". A lot of parents are tired by the tantrums children throw and they usually give in and get the child whatever he or she wants.

Actually it is the child's birthright to demand for things. But it is the parent's duty to decide what demands are to be met. Many times we feel that by giving the child things we are doing good parenting. Often it gives the wrong message to the child that his demands are right and so must be met. A child is in no way aware of the cost of things or its value, so when he just sees something on the telly or in the shops, he desires to own it. Every time the child cries or makes a little noise about getting the thing and the parent buys him the same, a message goes to the child that after crying for a little while he always gets the things he wants. Now who is responsible for this? Obviously we as adults are! In fact when giving things to children we never think of the long term consequences. We always think about short term goals i. e. giving pleasure to the child and making him stop from making a scene.

It is definitely not wrong to love one's child and shower him/her with gifts. But many times parents end up bringing too many things of the same type which the child does not really want. Also the child thinks that by throwing a major tantrum and making demands he is showing the "right behavior". Children learn from their own experience which often teaches them how to throw major tantrums. There are parents who give and buy things for their children not out of the love but out of sheer embarrassment because the child is screaming at the roadside, or rolling on the floor, or crying at the top of his/her voice. Many children also indulge in a lot of head banging or they hit others, bite parents or may be destructive by throwing things around during their tantrums. This also scares the parents and they prefer to then make the child quiet by giving into his demands. An older child may refuse to do homework, to eat or to talk with parents when throwing a tantrum. They obviously do things to get the attention of their parents.

The parent gets angry, irritated and may hit the child when he/she is throwing a tantrum but the child does not budge from his demand. Parents then feel bad for hitting the child and ultimately give into the demand. That time it is very difficult for parents to control their emotions. Hence the best thing to do when the child is screaming is to leave the child and go to the next room or just walk out of the shop if it is in a marketplace. Give the child time to understand that nobody is paying attention to him, before peeping back to see whether the child is alright.

As parents are the ones who have led the child to believe that all things he demands will be given, then it is the duty of parents only to see to it that they remain firm on their decision of not giving into the demands. Every parent should decide which demand of the child is right and which can be met. Sometimes it so happens that the parent may not give into the child's demands but somebody else like an uncle or an aunt or a grandparent would do so. Hence if mummy doesn't buy the chocolates, granny will definitely do! Most often parents and grandparents don't see an eye to eye on parenting and hence it is always necessary that all the members in the family discuss about the child's behavior and the strategies to control the same.

When parents and grandparents do not give into the unjust demands, the child gets the message, and stops the tantrums. It requires a lot of patience on the parent's side for expecting the change which would take place over time and not overnight. Talking to the child about his requirements, needs, praising him and giving him incentives for good behavior would eventually make the child happy and reduce the demands he makes. Children feel most happy on winning a prize; hence a small incentive does wonders for their morale. A collective effort by all members of the family would ensure that tantrums reduce and peace prevails in the house, which is essential for a healthy environment.

Another problem which is commonly seen in children is "Oppositional Defiant disorder". In this disorder children are defiant, back answer or argue with adults, are stubborn and at times aggressive and vindictive. They often deliberately do opposite of what is asked of them. Most of these children are known as 'difficult' children as they are very argumentative towards their parents and teachers. Many times parents don't realize it is a problem and hence continue to bear all the atrocities of the children without realizing that there are treatment options available for the same.

Vinay was a 7 years old child who would often refuse to help his mother if she asked him to do something saying that "it was not his job". He would get angry to the extent that it would appear as if he hated his mother. He would come home saying that others were not nice to him, he would keep on blaming them and his mother always had a hard time to controlling him. All days would end with a similar pattern with Vinay being beaten up and the entire home atmosphere being tense. Vinay was referred from his school for behavioral problems to the child guidance clinic. Going over the details of the history from the mother and the teachers report it was evident that Vinay has oppositional defiant disorder.

The treatment of this problem is 'parent training'. An orientation of parents to attitudes and emotional issues in children, disciplining, handling one's (parents) own emotions will go a long way in improving the child's behavior and the parent child relationship.

It is also important to discuss with parents about faulty role modeling e. g. where the child sees his parents behaving in a similar fashion. Harsh parenting or being too disciplined will also make the child rebellious. It is important that there is an emotional relationship between the parent and the child and this bond of attachment is further strengthened by communication.

Using the technique of star charting for good behaviors and giving incentives to the child for the appropriate behavior acts as reinforcement and lays the foundation for change in behavioral patterns.

12 *It Is Boring To Study*

"Urvashi cannot be sent down to play as she has to study" told her mother to me, when Urvashi was sent from her school for having difficulty in studying and failing. When I enquired into Urvashi's daily pattern of studying her mother reported that she had morning school and came home at 1. 00 p. m. Then she did her homework, went for classes at 3. 00 p. m. She would come back by 5. 00 p. m. do her homework from her class and then her mother would take her studies for some time. By then, it would be too late to go down to play and so she would see some T. V., eat dinner and go to sleep.

She was now in the VIII grade and her mother felt that she should be able to study for a few hours at a stretch so that her tenth grade studies would not be a problem. The entire day's sequence was quite horrific. The poor child spent more than 10 hours in doing studies and if she slept for 10 hours, that left only 4 hours for other activities.

What is the state of mind of parents of today? They have forgotten that child hood is a period of fun and frolic. There have to be studies but there should be a definite time allotted for play or recreation. How boring just to study and study! Obviously, children are going to be put off by the word STUDY . . . itself! Would we like it if the tables were reversed and we were made to go through this strenuous regime? Everywhere in the world a person works for 7 hours only, after which his overtime starts for which they get incentives and additional pay. Unfortunately our children are perpetually doing an "overtime of studies' with no incentives or breaks. Isn't that unfair?

And how much do you think would go into that stressed out brain, whenever one sits down to study? One is attentive for the first 40 minutes only, after which the attention starts wavering and the mind refuses to concentrate. Hence, one should take a break of 5 to 10 minutes where one can listen to music, read a paper or a novel, hum a tune and stand in the balcony etc. to relieve the mind. Studies can then be restarted. Studying regularly for 1 hour a day is enough. One does not have to keep studying continuously for good marks. But if one goes to several classes and has to do a lot of homework then, children invariably run short of time.

No wonder then, the commonest problems children have are lack of interest and concentration in studies, difficulties in understanding, increase irritability and sometimes fear of exams. As children have difficulty in completing their portion for exams, they often are tensed about their exams and always associate with exams in a negative way like being scared of them, having poor self-esteem and confidence.

It is therefore necessary that parents make academics interesting so that the child would want to study. It just takes a little effort on part of the parent to make the whole lesson easy to understand and learn. Visual learning is easy to memorize and remember than just hearing it or reading it. Hence when the subject matter is supplemented with pictures as in encyclopedias or with the information provided on the net then children develop interest in the subject. Today as information is available at the click of the button parents should inculcate e-learning. Children then get an entire perspective of whichever subject they want to learn.

Also it is important to make a reality based time table for the child which is practical to follow. Just studying round the clock is not efficient learning. Another important aspect is to assess the child's intelligence and then to tailor one's expectations as a parents accordingly. Give your child love and support and do not reprimand about not studying enough. There can be no end to how much to study for one can spend an entire life time learning! Hence study with your child so that you can make his understanding and learning easier. Always remember learning is a two way process. The more you share, the more it will be understood and reproduced and the child will not find his/her studies boring!

13 *Not Doing Well At School*

We just understood about making studies interesting for children. Sometimes parents find that their child has been repeatedly failing despite being sent to tuitions or being taught by the parents. Then one would have to look at the overall development of the child. It may happen that the child is developmentally delayed and is mentally challenged. The most common way to find out whether the child is having developmental delay is to look at his growth chart. Children are continuously developing till they are 18 years old. There are various milestones from birth onwards which have to be achieved which indicate to a parent whether the child is normal or is lagging behind.

Hence, details about when the child achieved his motor milestones like sitting, stranding, walking, running etc. are important. His language milestones would include when he started talking, how many words he can say, whether he can speak sentences or recite a song. Similarly whether he used to smile, respond, mix with others, could do things by himself give an idea about his social development. Some illnesses in childhood like encephalitis, hydrocephalus, meningitis or epilepsy hamper the normal development of the child which then results in intellectual disability. It is necessary to do the IQ of the child to ascertain the severity of the same. The grades of intellectual disability are as follows:

GRADE	IQ Range		
Mild	50 to 55	-	65 to 70
Moderate	35 to 40	-	50 to 55

Severe	20 to 25 - 35 to 40
Profound	Below 20-25
Slow Learner	70 to 90
Average IQ	90 to 100

Once the IQ and adaptive capacity /functioning of the child is ascertained then the parents can be counseled whether a child can learn in normal school or he/she requires some learning aids. Usually moderate mentally retarded children have to be sent to special schools, whereas severe and profound mentally retarded children will be unable to learn anything and will have to be looked after. Children who are mildly retarded however can do well in normal school with additional inputs.

It may also happen that at times children are average in their intelligence but are still failing repeatedly. This could be due to specific learning disabilities which would then have to be evaluated. Many times children are found to write illegibly, make a lot of mistakes while writing e. g. no punctuation, grammatical errors, spelling mistakes, letter reversals e. g. 'b' for 'd', 'p' for 'q' etc. as a result of which they score less. But when they are asked the same answer orally they can answer well. This problem is called as 'dysgraphia' and is often noticed when the child is 9-10 years old and written tests are the mode of examination.

The other most common learning disability is 'dyslexia' or 'reading difficulty'. These children have difficulty in reading lessons as there are a lot of omissions and grammatical mistakes. They do not know where to begin and where to stop and hence their comprehension of the subject may be poor. Arithmetical problem is another area in which the child may be poor as he makes silly mistakes while computing the problems and does not understand the symbols.

When a child is found to be having a learning disability on testing, then the treatment required is 'remedial education'. Just sending the child for tuitions does not help. Also the school authorities should be informed so that the necessary benefits can be made available to the child. No child should be segregated or made to feel that there is something wrong with him. Every parent should give their child the best they can without feeling burdened. Most important is to accept the problem and the child without any after thoughts. Ultimately if the parent can stimulate his child and be positive at least a part of the problem can be overcome.

14 *Sleepless Nights*

 A day in every household ends usually with a late night with all the members of that household engaged in some or the other activity. The father comes home late by 10. 00 p. m. or so. The grandparents and the rest of the family may be busy watching T. V. The kids may be finishing off their homework, waiting for their mother to call them for dinner. Most families may reserve the dinner time for a family meal where all members gather around but unfortunately the time is set around 10 to 10. 30 p. m. which is very late. Sometimes people finish off their meals by 9. 00 p. m. but are then engaged in doing various activities and the sleeping time is delayed up to 11. 00 to 11. 30 p. m. which is very late. All this has its toll on the next day functioning and more important is that no one has a refreshing sleep.

So caught up, are we, in our own events that time management has become a total failure in our households. Many parents keep on saying that their children don't sleep and are very active and energetic till late in the night and hence parents compulsorily put off the lights at midnight so that the child sleeps. Well, that's what one would expect in the households of such energetic parents. Children role model on their parents behavior and if parents are late sleepers then their children would also be the same. This raises a basic question. Is sleep really important?

If you ask any doctor or a stress consultant or a pediatrician, they would all say that adequate sleep is necessary for a good emotional and physical health. Sleep is that physiological state of the body when all the organs take rest and function at a lowered pace and this is necessary to prevent the bodily malfunction. Most of all the problems arise because the sleep is not adequate and the first symptom in many emotional problems is sleepless nights.

A good night's sleep i. e. about 10 hours refreshes the mind and body, rejuvenates and gives one energy and spirit to do things. It makes a person feel good which then has an impact on the various activities that one does during the day. Many children sleep late but get up early for the morning school. This makes them irritable and they have attention and concentration problems in school. Several families eat late that is beyond 10 pm and hence children go to sleep late. Such lifestyles will definitely have an impact on the sleeping habits of the entire families. Some children go to play after 9pm as they come from tuitions late. In all this the duration of sleep gets compromised and many times parents do not realize the effects of disturbed or decreased sleep on the growing up kids. If the child is supposed to sleep for at least 10 hours then today many children accept 6-8 hours sleep as a norm.

Children may have nightmares, night terrors or several other sleep related phenomena like sleep walking, sleep talking, head banging in sleep, moving their legs in bed or grinding of teeth. Depending upon the frequency of these episodes treatment can be given. It is also important to look into other factors that could be causing nightmares. Parental education on the need for sleep and the development of the child has to be emphasized so that faulty role modeling by parents can be corrected.

Right diet, good exercise or play with some discipline will go a long way in improving the child's sleep.

15 *Hyperactive Kids*

Aryan's parents came to me and just started crying. Aryan was a 12 year old boy studying in one of the good schools in Mumbai. But lately he had been stopped from attending school. His parents were summoned by the principal and were told that he would not be kept at school since he disturbed the class and was very mischievous. Currently Aryan was in the seventh grade. Up to fourth grade he was a ranker with 92% marks and now since the last two years he had deteriorated to about 40% marks in his sixth grade. His parents could not understand his deterioration nor could his teachers.

The only significant change in him over the last 3 years was that Aryan had become extremely distractible, and very fidgety. In the school, his teacher's complaints were that every 5-10 minutes he would get up and walk in the class or in the corridor and hence disturb the class teaching. All the other students would then start talking and not pay attention and the teacher would find it difficult to control the class. If he would not be moving, Aryan would constantly fidget on his bench, open the drawers, talk to his friends or sometimes pinch and hit them. This made it impossible for all teachers to teach their subjects as a result of which the school took a harsh decision of not allowing him to enter the class.

On listening to the entire account and observing the boy in the child guidance clinic, I came to the conclusion that he had "Attention Deficit Hyperactivity Disorder". This disorder is usually diagnosed in a child after 5 years of age when he is found to hyperactive and continuously on the 'go', fidgety, restless, impulsive and in attentive. Usually these symptoms should be present in two different situations for e. g. at home, or school or shopping malls etc. and there should be a complaint not only from the parents but also friends, family and the school teacher that the child is difficult to control.

Normally a child who is 2 to 3 years old has an enormous energy which gets expended by the little one moving about in the house. This is "physiological hyperactivity" which is a part of the child's development. Children start settling down and by the time they are in first standard, the hyperactivity reduces. However, if it persists to the extent that the child is very restless or accident prone or does dangerous things like jumping from heights, climbing windows etc. then the parent should consult a psychiatrist. The other important symptoms that are seen with hyperactivity are inattentiveness and impulsivity. Here the child would have difficulty in concentration, he would often be losing his pencils, erasers, water bottles in class, not answer on calling out once, have difficulty in focusing in play or studies or would be involved in various game activities at the same time. These children also have a high amount of impulsivity i. e. they would leave your hand and run across the road, answer questions out of turn, would interrupt when 2 people were talking etc. Some of these children may also have behavioral problems like fighting with others or abusing children to the extent that they become unpopular and others refuse to play with them.

As in Aryan's case, I got a report from the school teacher of his behavior and his parents after which Aryan's treatment plan was decided. These children require medication to control this excess 'energy' which has to be taken on a long term basis with breaks given during school holidays. As the focus is on the child's studies the drug dose is adjusted as per the school timings so that the child benefits from the medication and is able to concentrate in class. Teachers are also requested to let the child sit on the first row so that he is under the teacher's supervision and is less distractible. Behavior therapy like 'star charting' can be made use of where the child gets rewarded for good behaviors which act as incentives to improve the child.

ADHD children are called as 'toofan mail' (superfast train) and hence it is not difficult to miss them. Nevertheless as parents one has to be alert to pick up these changes which may seem normal but are not. An early remedy goes a long way in causing remission of symptoms rather than let the illness progress. To make the 'toofan mail' (superfast) to a 'mail' (slow) is definitely not a task impossible!

16 *Drama—Fun In Life*

Children are always a curious and creative bunch. They are always indulged in play whilst growing up, whether real or imaginary. So children are very prone to be good actors. They often see something on T. V. and try to enact it. Hence they can imitate their parents, teachers, friends and favorite actors. The acting world for them is full of fun and joy. It is a place where they can fight with bad men, have super powers, do things like jumping from sofas, playing warriors etc with wild abandon.

This is an important aspect of growing up as the child is going through the stages of social, emotional and intellectual development. Hence play acting helps him in all the stages of development. Many children are heard talking to themselves, as they utter dialogues, or tell jokes etc. when they are alone especially in the age group of 5-8 years. They become embarrassed or conscious if an adult enters the room but if left to themselves they can play the whole day, without having the need to talk to someone. This attribute of the children can be made use of in dramatics. They give the right expressions and say the right dialogues. This is because their thinking is such that they get into the 'role' without having to tell them. Hence it is easier to make children act than adults.

Of course there are other things which are also important. Like for e. g. if the child is shy or inhibited he will not open up in front of an audience, but when alone will be an amazing actor. Making the child comfortable, not focusing on the child's faults, not pushing him to do anything, but rather being with him, supporting him, acting with him or at times saying the dialogues with him would definitely help him get over his inhibitions. Hence, the child's temperament, the atmosphere at home which is positive and supportive help in nurturing the child and bringing out his best abilities.

Some children are very expressive. They will talk dime a dozen, sing a song or and break into a dance at the snap of your fingers. These children are performers and they are very "attention seeking". In fact they will demand that you hear them out. Hence if children with such a temperament are given a stage, they will definitely perform to the best of their ability. Parents have to understand their children and then put them in the appropriate creative classes whether it is drama, painting, singing or dancing. Just pushing children into everything confuses the child as his likes and dislikes are still to be formulated and he just goes to the classes not for his own interest but for his parent's satisfaction.

Dramatics is a very live creative art where you get into the 'role' and live that role forgetting yourself. It may be the most difficult thing to do—to stand in front of so many people and just enact keeping your own emotions aside. So you tell a joke to which the audience laughs but as an actor you keep a straight face. Hence it lets you forget your own problems as you don't bring them into picture and you get relief from stress. This is the best catharsis that can happen and should be used by people in their daily lives to help them overcome their own problems.

Dramatics therefore can act as a big stress-buster where sometimes by enacting your own problem you may overcome it or find a solution. Encouraging children to act will also help in their overall development like in helping language formation, diction, clarity of words, improving their self confidence, self esteem, helping them cope with their inhibitions and contributing as a major stress buster in their day to day activities. These children learn to interact with adults, other children, are able to put their thoughts across and of course continue learning through the varied experiences around them. It is a continuous lively world, a thing which children experience with great feelings and interest.

Today however the entire focus is not on learning the art but on cashing on it. Participation in competitions has increased to such an extent in all creative areas of talent search especially singing and dancing that T. V. channels are competing with each other for their reality shows be it for adults or little ones. Children are promised big prizes and given a lot of adulation and praise and attention and so the focus is more on performance and getting it right rather than the process of exploring, learning and enjoying. Parents too are supportive and want their child to do the best and it may result in putting a lot of pressure on the child.

Everything takes in own time and course in order to achieve professional standards. It is not a 2 months or a 2 year course. It is the amount of effort put in by the student which will give him the experience, the knowledge and the ultimate pleasure of mastering any talent. Hence sometimes competitions give you quick fame but unfortunately take away the learning experience. The field of dramatics has just entered the reality shows. It is important that children get opportunity to do the thing they like without being under continuous pressure that they have to win. Parents should also be aware of their expectations and not enforce it on children. If parents have the right attitude and let the child explore and enjoy, the child also learns the art properly.

Many parents feel that allowing the child to learn music, craft, art or dance is a waste of time, effort and money as they give importance only to academics. As parents we should remember all these creative abilities are a mode of expression of one's self-thoughts, feelings and behavior. Hence if I am happy, it will be expressed in my song, dance or art. The vibrancy of colors and voice would be evident to all.

Unfortunately we are taught not to express, hence we keep our feelings to ourselves so as not to let the outside world know and this is what we teach our child too. This is wrong because for a proper development we have to express and get a feedback on the same from others. All of us have some or the other talent presumably which we have hidden or which is yet to be discovered.

As parents let us allow our children to spread their wings and reach for the stars. The flight up is itself a big exhilaration rather than getting the stars. Let the child express and as a parent let us be aware that the child is expressing his inner feelings through some or the other medium—let the journey be a gradual one so that reaching the destination is an enjoyable process.

Teen Times . . . .

This section is on adolescents, their identity, their views on independence, mobile phones, sex education, pocket money, fashion, addiction, falling in love, career choice etc which the parents find difficult to deal with.

17 *Identity And The Crises*

Adolescence has been described as a period of storm and stress and it has been difficult to describe the start or the finishing point of adolescence, as physical or pubertal maturation which are considered as 'markers' for adolescence occur at different ages. One of the important aspects of adolescence is the thinking which changes. Many parents will recognize that in this phase the child now argues and counter argues and will formulate his own ideas and concepts which he expects to be followed.

What most parents don't realize is that as development occurs apart from physical growth there is also development in the way the world is seen, the pros and cons of a situation, comparing and analyzing the situation etc. which happens at the time when children are in the age range 12-18 years and use the feature of "abstract reasoning". It is due to this ability to abstract that the adolescent thinks about various possibilities, reflects upon them, deduces answers and arrives at conclusions.

This is very different from 7-11 year olds who generally follow what is told to them and abide by rules. That is why the 7 year old will always feel that teacher had told the answer to be such and such and will not believe their mother who tells the same thing. On the other hand, the adolescent who now has the ability to abstract realizes that the teacher and the parent are telling the same thing but in a different way.

But this ability to think also makes adolescents have their opinions on morality, friendships, responsibility and ideology. They also know that it is this thinking which causes increased self consciousness and introspection. This then helps them to develop their own sense of identity. In this stage another thing which will be observed by parents is "egocentrism" which means that the child is so self absorbed, and only feels that he is right or he only lives for himself, i. e. does activities for self, does not consider siblings or parents and is out rightly selfish.

This preoccupation with self is almost as if there is an imaginary audience with a sense of being on show. The adolescent carries out private experiment with this imaginary audience by trying to elicit a more predictable response from others in the outside world. This kind of rehearsal which the adolescent does mentally eventually allows a greater self awareness and degree of control over the environment which is a part of growing up.

It always takes time for children to form a consistent representation of themselves. Even at 14 & 15 years children will give self contradictory self descriptions, as if they do not know their 'real self'. It is only with time that they become aware and this happens with the influence of peers, family and school environment.

Most parents feel that children go through identity crises and they are not wrong. Identity crisis is the phase in adolescence where the young person struggles to decide who he or she is and wants to become. In fact it may be seen in adults also if their development has not been proper. What is identity? Identity is actually a perception of self with ideals. Identity development continues through adolescence and is a lifelong process. The process has been described by many and the 4 types of identity status are as follows.

1] Identity diffusion:—In this state there is a tendency to avoid commitment or decision making.

2] Identity foreclosure:—In this state there is a tentative acceptance of the views of others e. g. parents.

3] Moratorium:—A state of crises with active attention given to major decisions with exploration of possibilities but no firmly resolved commitments.

4] Identity achievement:—In this state the crises is resolved and firm commitments are made to ideals and plans.

Adolescents who are identity achievers are found to be better adjusted than others in many of the social situations. As the adolescents are in the process of development of the identity, families styles have a tremendous impact for e.g. like diffusion appears when there are rejecting or detached families. Foreclosure occurs when families are child centered, orthodox or conformist whereas moratorium and identity achievement are associated with warmth and support, encouragement of initiative and independence.

As you sow, so shall you reap holds true when parents say that their children are troublesome and have made life difficult. As long as parents are comfortable with the phase of adolescence and do not consider it to be a battle ground to be won, children will develop the right sense of identity and social cognition with responsiveness in the relationship with the parent and this supportive and challenging discussion of issues is associated with more advanced reasoning. As age advances, the ability to resolve the conflict develops and the conflict becomes better managed.

The parent should let the child explore the possibilities of the future instead of making him/her feel trapped and they should not let their anxieties come in the way of their child's development. This bonding between the parent and the child will ensure that there is identification with the parents' values and will create a continued warmth and responsibility in the parent child relationship.

18 *Peer Pressure*

Ｎone of us can lead a solitary life. We all need people around us to communicate, share and maintain relationships. We also are more comfortable amongst people who are of the same age group or who share certain qualities or likes and interests with us. These individuals form our "peers" and it may be that we may get influenced by them.

This has been seen in all our phases of development. Even as tiny tots, we may have had some friends who were special from whom we could not separate and some who were friends but with whom there was no much attachment. Human beings tend to form 'groups' of likeminded people. Even animals move in groups and it is therefore necessary to be a part of a body of people. At home this group gets called as the 'family unit' but it is a group of different ages and habits that a person desires.

Hence to be with peers and to live with them has always been a way of sustenance in the animal kingdom. For a group to function there has to be a 'group leader' whom the other members respect and relate to. This group is one where the members of the group interact with each other and are interdependent. Groups may be formed on the basis of age, interests, activities, similarity of members etc. An individual may behave differently as a part of the group and when he is alone. Groups share certain features that affect their functioning like 'norms' about suitable behavior 'responsibilities' to certain members, a 'communication structure' that reflects who talks to whom and a 'power structure' that determines which members wield the most influence. Thus in a 'teen group' a person who is credible, expert, trust worthy, likeable, physically attractive or rich may be relatively more effective than the other members in causing an attitude change.

Most teenagers start 'identifying' with the group next to their family. All their world starts revolving around group 'doings', group 'activities', group 'look'' etc. and they are constantly 'idolizing' their group. You may suddenly find them sporting a beard, keeping hair long or piercing ears in order to keep up with the 'image of the group'. Of course the message is quite clear—It is "we are somebody" and the individuality is lost. This is the reason why some of the children may blindly follow their friends without thinking.

Some of the group behaviors may be dangerous like exposure to drugs, alcohol, gambling and even going to sex workers. The age is such that everything is a 'game' and a new found independence with an attitude change is responsible for certain behaviors which the parents don't find appropriate.

Of course, all groups may not have a bad influence and there may be some groups which are called the 'study groups' where there is 'group thinking' i. e. individuals try to see that each member in the group progresses and they help each other. Hence many children find that they can study better with friends as issues can be discussed and most important is that they feel secure and comforted. Thus groups end up giving a lot of emotional and moral support to their members which is beneficial for the child's growth.

So 'peer pressure' can work both ways. It may have a 'good influence' and you may suddenly find your child behaving properly, listening to you, showing more understanding etc. if he belongs to a group which understands these values or if it is a 'bad influence' then your child may become more rebellious, more defiant, aggressive and demanding because his group may be believing in those 'principles'. As a parent, you should be aware of your child's group, their ideologies and their group cohesiveness. You should know how your child relates to his group and if he is particularly following any one group member. If you find that the child is behaving oddly or is doing things that are wrong you have every right as a parent to forbid him from being a part of that group.

Before you take on the parental role and just barge and tell him to stop going out with friends you will find that he does not listen. As most children identify strongly with the group, they cannot bear anyone calling their group any names. Hence in order to see that your child does not suffer or distrust you, it is necessary to communicate to your child your fears as well as understand his needs, so as to be able to tell him your view point.

You may even have to speak to his group members and confront them if you feel that their activities are not right. You will have to tackle the group as one, rather than saying that someone is a bad influence on him. You may also have to take the parents of the other children into confidence if you have a doubt on the group activities. Turning a blind eye or a deaf ear may cause irreversible damage. Therefore be forewarned and forearmed when your child is a part of a group.

19 *Pocket Money*

I was visiting one of my friend's when her 14 years old son came and said "Mom, I am not there for dinner. We are going for a movie and then some grub. Please give me 250 bucks. My friend quietly gave him the money and asked him to enjoy himself. There were no questions asked and no answers given. I was surprised. I asked my friend if she routinely gave him "pocket money" or money was given only when Rohan was going out . . . . Ant her answer had me stumped! For Rohan had a daily allowance of Rs. 50/—excluding the travel allowance as he went to school by public transport and the money he got daily could be spent on buying any eatables, CDs or anything that struck his fancy. Twice a month he and his friends would go for movies and eat outside. That amounted to anywhere between 250-500 rupees per outing. And did Rohan save any? Well the answer was an obvious—"No" for he had an ATM at home. My friend of course did not have any remorse over giving him the money. On the other hand she proudly told me—"well he just goes for movies. At least he is not smoking, drinking, going to the discotheques . . . . So what is wrong in giving him the money?" There were many things I wished I could tell her . . . . But then I did not.

"Pocket-money"—or daily or monthly allowance which was once upon a time given by parents to their children so that they could travel by bus, taxi or rickshaw in times of crisis and to buy the occasional vada-pav or samosa from the school canteen has long ago gone a drastic transition in today's media-savvy, culture-savvy world of attitudes and value systems. Of course prices of diesel and petrol have gone up to add to the woes and the value of the rupee has hit the bottom. Understandingly, the

Rs. 5 or Rs. 10 that sufficed 10 years ago, now had increased to Rs. 50 and Rs. 100 but was still insufficient.

One has to understand today, what message we are trying to give our children. Whether it is one has to work hard, so that a penny saved is a penny earned, and teach them what is saving money in a 'piggy bank' or to spend and enjoy oneself as times are changing and so our needs. There is a tremendous conflict amongst parents on these issues and 'peer pressure' makes the parents vulnerable as they give in to the demands of their children.

There is absolutely nothing wrong in the child going for movies, eating outside etc. But then as a parent you can teach them that eating out or going to the movies is acceptable once a month provided the child saves money for it. You want to give the child an allowance . . . . give it— but see to it that you are not giving him far too much. Most children go by school bus and are supposed to eat the lunch they carry from home or the meals provided by the school. There is no reason why they should eat a packet of Lays or 'batata wada' daily or drink a coke. If as parents, we allow him to do the above things then, it means we are consenting to this behavior and then we are only responsible for the same.

A 14 years old boy is supposed to be in school studying and not having Rs. 50/—in his pocket to spend on things advised by his friends. Giving easy money puts a child at risk of developing habits such as smoking, going to cybercafé and indulging in nefarious activities. Tomorrow the same child will demand Rs. 500/ day once he starts attending college. Are we then going to give him that money? All this business of giving "daily allowance" has sadly boomeranged on us parents. But despite this, we have not been able to wean ourselves from the societal pressures. Your child has to be made to understand that his primary needs of food, clothing and shelter are your responsibilities and anything done in excess of that is extravagance. Your child should be taught the concept of 'saving' and yes if you want to give him a pleasure trip, combine it with a motive—like his marks in the class test were better than last time or his teacher had not given him any negative remarks this month . . . . So he deserved a treat! You could celebrate by calling friends over and having specially prepared meals than indulging in pizza parties or Macdonald treats.

Money given easily loses its value and then there is no incentive to earn. let it be, that your child gets a minimal allowance and for frivolous expenses he has to achieve a target. He should get the message that 'he has to earn' that extra money he needs by doing certain things. As parents you can give him the target at the beginning of the month, and the money is given, only if the targets are achieved. Children may throw tantrums, become agitated and demanding, call you names, say that their friend's father was a better person than you . . . . But then remember you are the 'BOSS' and you as a parent have to lay down the rules. One does not have to be "authoritarian" but "authoritative" in the bargain to be a good parent.

20 *Difficult Teenagers*

 M any times as your child grows up there are several traumatic scenes at home which is the beginning of adolescence. Like your teenage daughter is taking forever in the bathroom (again), but you need her to get ready so you can get to your daily routine. Meanwhile, your child is going through agony by looking at her image in the mirror. She's distraught with the image that she has grown a pimple on her nose. Outside in the hallway, you start pounding on the door, yelling at her to hurry up. She screams, "God, you just don't understand! Leave me alone!" When she finally emerges, she gives you the silent treatment. You are left wondering, "Why doesn't my kid listen to me? Does she have to fight me on *everything*?"

Looking at you and your teen would reveal two different worlds, two different perspectives—and a giant disconnect that can make communicating a real mystery. The more you push your kids, the more defensive and defiant they get. Clamming up or exploding are ways your adolescent would attempt to manage his/her stress. That's because distancing and explosiveness are often the only ways your teen knows how to communicate when things get intense as they find a huge gap in understanding the parents perspective and hence feel that it is of no use to talk to his/her old man or woman.

Well as parents this is the biggest challenge we have to overcome. No matter how hard it might be, try to start all interactions with your child with understanding, even if you don't fully agree or even quite comprehend what they're talking about. Suppose your teenage daughter is not doing her schoolwork and preparing for her exams, and instead is online with friends chatting. It drives you crazy because you're thinking of her performance, future and goals in life whereas she is very much in the present wanting to patch up with her friend with whom she had a fight. Again these are two different worlds.

Perhaps as a parent one can take her emotions into consideration and start by saying, "I understand how difficult it is for you when you have a fight with one of your friends. I also know that you need to pass this test tomorrow. Schoolwork is your job and it's your responsibility to do it to the best of your abilities. Let's sit down and think of a good way you can do your work and still make up with Malvika. Start from a place of understanding, and try to put yourself in your child's shoes first before telling her what needs to change. Also you can tell them about the fights you had with your friends and the tactics you used so that you "open your kids' ears." Instead of feeling like they have to defend themselves against you, they actually listen, cooperate and follow your advice.

Parents usually get emotional when arguing with their teen and this creates problems. You may not like how he's behaving—or even how he's thinking—but keep your emotions out of it, even if his behavior affects you. It's a skill every parent should learn where everything your teen says should not be taken personally. There's actually no reason to be mad at your child for being himself. He may be making a poor choice, but the truth is, he might not yet have the skill set to make a better one. So your job is to help and guide him to better choices so he can in turn develop a better skill set. When you realize what your job is as a parent, it will help you be less emotional and not let your frustrations distress you. After all it's part of the parenting business.

It is important to make your child feel that he has intelligence and some great ideas. Let him see that you believe in him and that you're not mad at him for struggling in his life. When you let him see that you have faith in his abilities and he has the space to work things out on his own, you will begin to develop true confidence in him. Don't ask questions that put your child on the defensive like, "Why can't you get up on time? What's wrong with you?" This always results in a monologue with you berating and he putting a pillow on his head. Instead, try opening a conversation with, "Raju, do you have any ideas for how you might get up on time?" If he says he doesn't know, offer a few of your own and ask which one would work for him. Let your teen know that his problems are his to solve. You should be there to help him figure out solutions— and to let him deal with the natural consequences of his behavior. Also remember don't end up criticizing him. Appreciate his answers and help him find his own way.

Your goal is to help your child think for himself, which will in turn help him feel like he has some control over his world. Listen openly to what he says and ask him to think critically about each choice. What will work and what will be problematic about each decision? What would be the natural consequences of each choice—and how would he feel about dealing with that?

There is neither any battle to be won when you are having an argument with your child nor do you have to show your superiority as a parent. If your child is acting out, that's his problem. Your problem is to decide how you will choose to behave toward him. If he is screaming at you don't retaliate but just walk away. Let him know you won't talk with him until he can approach you with civility. You have to be firm as a parent and not tolerate "rude" behavior. Also it gives you a chance to think over the situation. Your child will also be less defiant because he will have no one to resist. Another rule of thumb is to avoid doing anything until you and your child have both calmed down. When things are quiet, you can sit down and talk with him. It's never good to try to bring up a difficult subject or resolve a conflict in the heat of the moment. So if either you or your child is upset, take a break, go somewhere and come back when you can address things in a calmer way.

If you attempt a conversation with your child and he's rude or out of line, that's when you have to hold on to yourself and make sure you don't get dragged into a fight. If your relationship with your child is such that it's impossible to have an open, respectful conversation at this point in time, remember that it's still your job to stay firmly planted. You don't sulk because your child is already sulking. Parenting therefore is one of the most trying jobs when handling teenagers.

Remember just being open to your teens feelings and having mutual respect will improve the parent child communication dramatically.

21 *Teen Talk: Sex Education*

When the child comes of age and shows physical signs of developing into a man or woman, as is evident from the change of voice, developing acne, beard / moustache and growth of hair over armpits and the pubis, it brings along with it new emotions over this development. There is tremendous uncertainty in the boys and girls as they try to cope with a new look. Shame, embarrassment, guilt, happiness joy etc. may be the varying shades of emotions experienced as they go through this phase of accepting change. Obviously, they feel extremely uncomfortable to discuss these uncertainties with their parents.

As the breasts start budding in a girl, she experiences tenderness over the breast area. But very few girls would actually go and tell their mother so! Isn't that sad? A child finds it difficult to express to those who have bred him. One of the reasons for this is that in the Indian culture, sex is definitely taboo subject. Not many parents are comfortable talking about genital organs and their functions, if at all, a mother may only tell her daughter about 'menarche' that is onset of menstruation but still she is incapable of preparing her for the process.

Most often, the parents themselves have a limited knowledge of sex organs. In fact the children may be more knowledgeable due to a lot of information being available on the internet but the emotional aspect has to be dealt by parents. There is nothing wrong in imparting information to our children. After all, let them learn it the right way, rather than experiencing it through other people's advice and landing into trouble.

Although teens and parents may communicate about certain topics, if you were to ask a group of 13-18 year-olds the question, "Do you discuss sex openly with your parents?" You may be surprised at the low number of "yes" answers you hear. Teens mean different things when they say they talk openly about sex with their parents. One definition of open communication is whether teens have *conversations* (rather than get lectured) with their parents about contraception, sexual behavior, and sexually transmitted infections/diseases (STIs/STDs)? And the answer is an obvious No!

However parents who grew up during the sexual revolution of the late 1960s through 1970s may be better able to communicate about sex, based on their own values and past experience than they could have with their own parents who grew up before the sexual revolution. India being a diverse culture with several religious practices, sex is hardly a dinner table conversation. Parents don't bring about the topic as many parents have had an orthodox upbringing. Hence sex education being done at home in today's era is still a wish to come true!

Obviously, if these teens are not talking with their parents about sex, then who are they talking to? Well it is their peers who are the sources of information. Though schools now do take sex education it is usually factual information. The questions running through a teenager's mind would be the practical advice on how to apply the information he/she has learnt. Sadly most schools lack in doing this. Hence sex education should not just be the responsibility of schools, communities, or the media. The best sexual health education begins at home with the parents communicating their own values on sexuality with their teens and understanding their teen's perspective as per their teenager's stage of development, life experience, personality and knowledge.

Many parents are embarrassed to talk about sex as they feel their child is more knowledgeable about sex than they actually are. Also today's teens feel that their parents are close-minded, uncompassionate or not clued in to the problems faced by them. Hence they do not find it worth discussing with them. If at all a girl would discuss issues related to menstruation with her mother. Boys rarely have a man to man talk with their fathers in our country, as most men feel inhibited to talk on this subject. Also many parents feel that talking openly on the subject would make the child curious to venture into romance, which is again very much disapproved in the Indian subcontinent.

Ultimately, educating teens about sexuality needs to be a balance between what teens want to learn about and what we as adults feel they need to know to develop into healthy adults. Parents can effectively communicate with and educate adolescents by encouraging open communication, using accurate yet simple names for body parts, sexual behaviors, and feelings.

It is very important for parents to be non-judgmental. They should disagree respectfully, making suggestions rather than directives ("you should"). Parental values and moral expectations about sexual behavior should be clearly communicated rather then left to the child's imagination. It is the parent's duty to tell the child about sexual and other risk behaviors like unprotected sex, potentially harmful sexual relationships, depression, anxiety etc. One should also be alert to changes in our child's behavior due to the hormonal influence.

Overall, keep in mind that communicating effectively about sexuality with adolescents has important, positive long term benefits—those which promote the teen's physical, social, emotional and mental health. A sexual experience is an intense emotional experience. Let your child know about it and if you are with him, he will trust your value systems. If we expect a change, we have to change a little our self.

22 *Staying Connected*

The concept of communication has increased by leaps and bounds in these last 10 years and the need to be 'constantly in touch' with a person is now the trend. So much so that when you are with the person you have nothing to say but once away, you get a craving to either talk to him or SMS him. I would say that it's a great thing communication is being sought as it is the way to improve our interpersonal relationships but, somewhere along the line this has got misinterpreted as "we can connect and communicate, only if we have a mobile". Gone are the days when friends would meet and chat over hours, catching up on each other lives. Now they do meet, but each is busy on his/her phone. There has been such a dramatic and drastic change in our lives where each one of us is now living in our own world of 'e-mails and SMS's' doing social networking with no actual contact with the 'living people'.

When adults are addicted to gadgets, can the children be far behind? Today, in each household everybody from servants, drivers to siblings carry mobile phones. Such is the change that a mobile phone is no longer considered a 'luxury item' but rather a 'necessity' of the day! In fact in order to be the best in communication everyone wants the latest apps in their gadgets to be better connected. The convenience of communication is definitely at the tip of your fingers and it has made our lives easy. Today, people feel disabled if there is no mobile. When, this is the scene globally how can one blame children who feel it is 'the thing' to have? Hence when the child graduates to VI grade and above, he/she demands very rightly for a mobile phone. Many parents also feel it is right to give the child one, as now the child is growing up, is responsible, has to attend several classes, may be late and so on and so forth. So the child is given the phone for calling home when leaving from classes or when the child is going to be late so that the parents do not worry. But in order to salvage the mother's preoccupation and anxiety about her dear one, the child unfortunately gets exposed to something as sinister as the mobile phone.

The mobile is used for far more other things than calling up the mother to tell her know that he/she would be late. Of course, there are parents who then try to keep tabs on who their child is calling or who sends messages etc. but then is it right? It would amount to invading privacy even if it is of your child. In the bargain the child learns mistrust instead of trust, all because of the 'mobile phone'.

Every parent should realize the potential hazards of any gadget before exposing their child to it and I am not only talking about the health hazards which have been proved but also giving the child unlimited freedom in his search for knowledge or communication which may then expose him to unneeded things way earlier in life. The content of the SMS messages which may not be age appropriate will also be read by him raising several doubts in his mind.

It is definitely not a necessity for a school going child to have a mobile. Your child has to be in a secure relationship with you before you battle out with him the pros and cons of the mobile. You will have a raging battle with him/her because all his/her friends may be having one. If your communication with your child is not via the mobile but face to face, it may not be difficult to explain your stand and also understand your child's viewpoint. After all, the role of a parent is to be a continuous guide and friend and one should see that one plays both the roles adequately rather than only one of them. A child will understand only if you talk to him as one rather than dictating rules because you are 'the parent'. The needs of the child should be addressed.

A growing up adolescent does require 'space' or freedom to talk to people he likes. Give him the security that you trust him when he uses a landline. Don't hover around to check whether it is a boy/girl he is talking to or for how long he is on the line. It would be preferable to have one separate land line installed in the home for the kids, so that it is 'their phone' for use. At least then, they would still be on the 'road' rather than on a 'runway' and 'brakes' can be easily applied before it is too late!

23 *Bad Company*

Come adolescence and the parents are already warned. Their young child has now stepped into his teens and is now behaving like a typical teenager. Their worries are often farfetched for now they feel that the child is going to do all the forbidden things like going to parties, disco, smoke, watch blue films etc. Parents do become over cautious and put tremendous restrictions on the child. To have fears about a growing up child is perfectly normal but as parents we should realize that the fears should be realistic.

In today's world of e-communication and media explosion the child has more knowledge and more sources of information than we did as children. Hence, parents should first of all improve their communication with their children. Rather than asking about school and the things taught by the teacher involve them in a one to one conversation of topics which interest them—you could discuss about movies, happenings, news, sex education, friends as also studies. Involve them, so that trust rules over mistrust. Your children should respect & look up to you but they should not be scared of you. The fear of parents may sometimes prevent the children from opening their hearts and mind to parents and thus parents may miss out on an important communication.

Nothing is good or bad at the outset. It is our perception of the situation which makes us feel so. Hence all your child's friends will be the same. They will be a curious, adventurous bunch of teenagers. If the values instilled in your child have been accepted by him and your role is of a friend, the child himself will come forth and tell you of friends who are unworthy. You do not have to hammer it to him that his friends are "bad". To achieve this level, there has to be mutual trust. Plenty of communicative parents have a habit of branding some people as good friends. The friends they call good are the ones who would be the quiet guys who sit in one corner and say, "How are you aunty?", they don't shout or laugh loudly, are generally obedient and non flamboyant children. On the other hand, those who are bad company, would be the ones who—giggle or laugh too much, the boisterous, outgoing types who spend too much, always party, talk for long on the phone and wear 'funny outfits' which challenges your modesty.

So as parents, you forbid your child from being too involved with them. Is it right? Who are we to decide everything for our children? We are parents true, but we can't be dictators. They should have the freedom to experience the joys and follies of friendship and moreover we should instill good faith and confidence in them about being a good friend. Yes, one does have to worry about certain things like if your child starts smoking, drinking etc. due to peer pressure. Then one has every right to dissuade the child from being friends with them. But then too, one would have to communicate to the child the problems that would ensue on continuing the friendship. A heart to heart talk always solves problems faster than giving mere orders.

As the outlook is changing, we may have to change certain of our perceptions. It may be difficult but certainly not impossible. If all the parents in the world, decide that their child has fallen in 'BAD COMPANY', imagine the 'number of bad people' each country would have produced and if for every good child there is a bad child, then 50% of the population would be called 'bad'. There are problem children who have certain bad behaviors but it is a part of a psychiatric problem for which help should be sought. Most of the children are normal growing teenagers who may be swayed by these problem children and may resort to bad behaviors due to peer pressure. But the incidence of this situation is small.

Hence if we talk with our children in their language we may be able to understand them better and then help them to understand us.

24 *Pub Culture*

"**M**om, please let me go. All my friends will be there, we are a group of ten, you don't have to worry. I'll be home by 10'clock latest". Well, these are the dialogues going on in every household, once the child has reached his teens and is experiencing his / her new found independence. The intense peer pressure and the need to be accepted by his/her group of friends is the only thing that matters to the teenagers. Most often, the child may not even know the implications of a particular action, but may be swayed by the group's decision. Every group has a group leader who influences the members of the group. The age is such that along with physical and hormonal changes, the individual also goes through intense emotional experiences, each of which forms his attitude and a change of behaviors.

There is an increased need to show the world that 'I am someone' and 'I have a mind of my own' with an obvious fact that 'I can look after myself' and 'I know what it right for me'. The age is of 'Me, Me & Only Me'. The intense self importance, need to defy rules and authority along with an adventurous spirit to 'try something new' often causes several sleepless nights for the parents. Most of the times, parents are at a loss to answer questions and feel helpless with the situation. At least 'allowing the child to go' does not disrupt the homely atmosphereor create a scene in front of the neighbors.

Of course getting permission gives the child 'a high' which then increases manifold in actually being in a forbidden place like the 'pub' and seeing the charged up atmosphere with very little 'breathing space' and a lot of body contact. Additional benefits include seeing fashionably dressed girls showing more flesh with a few drinks thrown in. For the young adolescent who is just experiencing the feelings of manliness and virility or a new found womanhood, going to the pub is enough to make him/her feel intoxicated. Then, as parents what should we do? Do we allow them or we don't? Do we trust them or we do not? Or do we buy time and say next year. But the time has surely come for us as parents to decide.

Let us be prepared as parents that our children are going to be making these demands. Over the years as the child reaches secondary school, either the parents should instill their value systems with the cultural upbringing by taking the children into confidence and telling them about likes, dislikes, dress sense etc. rather than suddenly exploding on them by saying 'I didn't expect this from you'.

If we allow our daughters to roam around in figure hugging tight clothes that reveal more of the body, the whole year through, it may not be right to suddenly tell her when she wants to go out, that the clothes don't seem right. It definitely may not be easy talking to headstrong teenagers. But one can't give up the responsibility. Since times are changing and with the advent of the fashion culture, pop music, hard rock, the genre of the young generation is far different from our own upbringing when we were children.

We may not be able to reconcile to the changing societal values and we have every right to have our own views but we should also look at the child's perspective. For him it may be dancing to abandon, having a great time and enjoying oneself. Our fears may not be related to the dancing but to the energy required to put in that effort which may make the young teen susceptible to down a few beers or red bulls! Also we may not be aware of his entire group of friends who may get drugs and mix them in their cocktails or mock tails. We realize and know what will happen when intoxicated—our teen may not—and so we come down heavily on him/her. Many things happen in the pub setting—there could be rave parties, there could be disinhibited behavior and undue consequences. Your child may be an innocent bystander who can get drawn into any controversy. Hence, even if your child says it's just going to be a dance— you will have to tell him/her the actual facts that happen at a pub.

Teenagers are at an impressionable age and are very much likely to be influenced by all that is happening around them. One definitely can't blame them for that! But then as a parent one does not turn a blind eye and say, 'I will tackle it when the time comes'—for today it is the fourteen year old who wants to go to the discotheque every weekend but tomorrow it may be a 10 year old demanding the same, for children are growing up too fast, before their normal expected ages. Therefore, today a school going boy has already had an experience of smoking, drinking and yes, even going to the commercial sex worker. All this spells 'DANGER' for us parents and we all will be helpless as we can't fight the society which is being influenced.

But, at least let us not be scared. Let us think in advance. Let us talk to our children about 'things happening in life'. Let it be as "I had an experience in my childhood where . . . ." Let it not be as "I have never done this"; "you have brought shame . . . ."

Let us understand our children, let us share our fears. Let us talk clearly and not hesitate to do so. Let us take the first step . . . . our child will surely follow.

25 *Trend Setter*

The other day as I was going for my daughter's open house, I came across many of the youngsters, dressed in real trendy clothes. What was surprising was, their mothers were also sporting similar attire. If one goes to any of the fast food joints or malls in the city one will come across many such teenagers wearing clothes that probably would have threatened our modesty. Imagine an 8 inch piece of cloth wound around the torso with an expanse of the midriff to be displayed boldly—making a statement "It's my body!" All of us who are parents and trying to achieve sensibility in our young children are at a total loss as to how to handle this problem! Call it an influx of knowledge about beauty and fashion or increased media coverage of the rich and famous society members and their apparel which gets discussed and displayed every day. The range of cosmetics and accessories to accompany the dress code make an emphatic fashion statement which strongly influences the teenage population. Thus when there is so much exposure in today's times regarding 'what to wear', 'how to look beautiful' and 'have young attitude', that it often becomes a real testing time for parents. We definitely cannot stop this influence and the upcoming cultural change in value systems.

What would have to be inculcated in the minds of our children is that everything that's fashion may not look good on everyone. One has to be proud of one's physique and looks. It does not mean that one has to ape the fashion of the west or one's friends and wear clothes which do not suit us. The child has oodles of confidence to walk on the road and expose her body parts to one and sundry. All this talk would probably fall on deaf ears, as the youngsters go about their way, saying that their parents are old fashioned and living in middle ages than the 21st century.

But somewhere, the parents have to draw a line as to what kind of clothes their child can wear. You can still wear fashionable clothes which bring out your personality than do a cheap imitation. Of course now a day's youngsters try to earn money so that they can indulge in these accessories. They are free to earn and spend their money but it doesn't mean that they are mature and can decide on clothes which outrage modesty. There is already a debate raging on why should parents decide as the adolescent always feels "it is my body" and so" I will be the judge".

Hence as parents, I would say that one would have to talk to children about changing trends, inadequacies, fears, their self confidence and self esteem. Parents should also keep in mind that one cannot stop and prevent children from doing things all the time or else they will become rebellious and defiant. Parents are more scared of their children being designated as 'vulgar or cheap' due to their dress sense and more important no parent wants his or her daughter to fall prey to eve teasers or be molested which is very much on the increase in our country. A child can follow fashion and still see to it that the effect of the clothes does not tarnish his/her image.

Another important thing is that if parents themselves sport such kind of clothes which are clinging or revealing then the child accepts this as a norm as the mother approves of the dress code. The mother then cannot demand of her daughter to wear decent clothes. It is also seen that mothers like to dress their daughter in pretty dresses when the child is in the age range of 5 to 12 years and will feel proud at how 'cute' their daughters looks in strapless dress. However, when the child becomes '14' the same dress does not seem 'cute'. For a child who has been wearing tight T-shirts, showing her navel all through her growing up phase, this sudden transition of putting a stop to such clothes by her parents confuses her and she revolts. Of course, she is stepping into womanhood and is experiencing new feelings and desires and feels the need to have her own say.

The child's desires often clash with the parental wishes. Hence parents have to instill the values which they really believe in by telling their child and following those values themselves. A heart to heart talk and giving a nonjudgmental opinion on how their child looks in particular attire without being autocratic, demanding or harsh can go a long way in boosting the child's morale and confidence. One also has to keep in mind that the child may get influenced by 'peer pressure' to wear certain clothes, so as to be accepted by the group. This dilemma can be resolved if the parents tell the child that it is the qualities of individuals which bind people in a group rather than frivolous things like dress code, eat code etc.

Therefore 'BE A FRIEND' to 'HAVE A FRIEND' of your child.

26 *Love Is In The Air*

Anu's parents were saying that their 16 year old was nowadays talking a lot on the phone with boys and was often coming home late. On questioning her standard answer was "I am with friends". They claimed that they made enquiries and found from her friends that she was friendly with a boy from her classes and even bunked classes. Of course, they reported that they confronted her on those issues to which she replied that she was just friends with him and nothing more. Her parents could not talk to her further and so they came to me for guidance. They wanted me to intervene and tell her that she was young and should focus on studies and career and not love or romance. They didn't approve of the boy and were not sure of his character or living status. I listened to them patiently as they went on saying how ashamed they were of their daughter's behavior or how no one in their family has ever fallen in love. Their dilemma was evident. They were not sure of what was going to happen and how they were supposed to handle the situation. Also they were from a conservative traditional Indian background where being in "love" was not an acceptable behavior.

I would say that this is an extremely 'tricky situation' for any parent to be in and my sympathies are with all these parents who have to strive and control the situation. As the child springs into the steps of woman hood and manhood he or she has to face a lot of bodily and emotional changes. In adolescence with the surge of hormones making you feel and look 'masculine' or 'feminine', the child has suddenly got to look after his or her own emotions.

The interest in the opposite sex is now in the fourth gear and the heart is rapidly racing to reach the end of the race. Yes in this age group of teenagers a new feeling blossoms which gets quenched by reciprocal feelings form the opposite sex. So one can't blame them if 'love is in the air' and our little ones are continuously breathing this air. As parents, I would say, that we have to be alert for these things to happen. Our child may get interested or start liking boys or someone more in particular. Nagging them continuously, harping about 'bad behavior' or 'this thing is not done' or 'you have brought shame to our family' is going to make matters worse. It will also take the child away from you as the child will now no longer communicate to you. The child will see the parent as 'the enemy' trying to take away the loved object. Hence most children refuse to listen to parents as they try to protect their interest.

It is therefore necessary, as parents not to express criticism about the 'loved objects' directly to the children. If the doors to communication are to be kept open in order to solve the issues, the parents should first understand the 'pangs of love' which are experienced by their children. Talking about togetherness, the 'emotion' called 'love', the experience of being in the company of the opposite sex, feelings of sensuality and sexuality would be more helpful in improving the child understanding and the parent, child relationship. A negative stand or preventing the child from going out or talking on the phone would not only deteriorate the existing parent child relationship but also make the child more rebellious. All this would then create more problems for the parent child relationship.

It is next to impossible to prevent 'love' from happening. It is next to impossible to prevent our children from 'growing up'. Hence, it is but natural to expect changes in relationship with that little dash of hormones. It is most important that we get down from the pedestal of parenthood and don the mantle of 'being a friend'. Adolescents need people to 'talk their language'. Parents usually end up being parents and are autocratic and authoritative. A little bit of discipline is needed but it should not end up as parental tyranny.

Let them fall in and out of love. Let them understand what relationships are. Explain to them that it is natural to like a person for, it is basic human instinct. A parent is scared of the child crossing boundaries. Tell them your fears and how to identify people who may take advantage of them. Remember the child in already in his or her 'love world'. If you try to destroy it you become 'Enemy No. 1'. You want to see that nothing in the world happens to them. For that you have to get accepted in their 'love world'. Take them into confidence; ask them to meet loved ones at home where they can talk privately in their rooms, rather than at the seashore or in the park. Learn to trust them, so that they end up trusting you.

The bubble of love may burst. But you should be there to comfort your child and not be the terminator. For even if we want to protect our child for life from any bad things, we as parents love our limitations! But nevertheless communicate with them . . . . as that is the key!

27 *Danger Zones*

We are all versed with the danger zones that we see on the telly in the various reality and competitive shows. It just goes to show that sometimes even the contestants are not aware about why they have gone in the danger zone and are at a risk of being evicted out from the reality show. Similarly as parents we may be unaware of what is happening to our children and whether they have gone into any "danger zones". For an adolescent growing up brings about a lot of changes in his body and mind. Girls start menstruating and due to hormonal influence a lot of sexual feelings come into play. Suddenly parents may notice that their daughter is dressing up, is very aware of fashion and is being influenced by the same. If they try to talk to her, they get an outburst of tantrums. Many adolescents are more close to their friends than their parents and follow the group culture.

Adolescents are a part of the peer group and hence they usually get influenced by the thoughts and actions of their friends. Hence as the society is getting very westernized and liberalized, parents are having no option but to allow their teenager children to have late night parties, go to movies, pubs etc. It is indeed going to be very stressful for the parent to keep a watch on the whereabouts of his/her child. Hence, most parents become authoritarian and prevent their children from going out. They usually set time limits and expect the child to come home by that time. They may also repeatedly call them on their mobiles. This results in a lot of resentment in the children who are going through a phase of having to prove their identity and independence. This may then result in `children hiding things from their parents or telling lies, stealing money for their expenses etc. A parent therefore first has to have such a relationship with the child that the child would seek the parents' opinion first instead of his/her friend. A father or mother should first be a friend and then a parent. In being a friend one would have to understand the feelings, attitudes and behaviors of the children which would be expected at that age and then we should act as a parent in trying to protect or care for our children or lay down the rules and regulations.

But what happens in most families is that we are very eager as parents to make our view clear and hence are very rigid in the rules. Hence our communication with our child is also in authoritarian and commanding tones. The child realizes that telling the parent anything will worsen the already strained parent child relationship and so they start hiding things or telling lies.

Having an adolescent daughter, who is growing up is a very stressful thought for a parent, who wants to protect the girl from any untoward harm. But the same parent is inhibited in telling his/her daughter about sex education. If the parent can speak to his/her daughter about his fears and give the children the knowledge of sex education and so that the child is able to protect herself then the child has no qualm in talking to the parent about his/her emotions. I would like to elaborate this with the examples below which would make the parent realize that their child is probably is in some "danger zone".

i] Rekha was a normal 15 year old girl going to a co-ed school. Her background was that she was raised in a very conservative and orthodox joint family where the women in the house did not speak to males. Rekha was a typical teenager in tenth grade who was more interested in friends than studies. There were a lot of restrictions put on her bringing her friends' home, going out etc. Rekha's friends gave her all inputs about what was happening around and she spent a lot of time in talking to her friends which included boys and girls after school. She started reaching home late and on being questioned she would say that there were extra classes in school for tenth. Her parents had put her for tuitions just across their house where they could watch her movements. Rekha's behavior changed and she started becoming aggressive, abusive and hostile towards her family members for which she was brought to the psychiatrist. She said that she felt like a prisoner because all her movements were watched.

Her brothers also would come to the tuition class to check if she was there. If any boy called up at her place, he was told it was a wrong number. She said that she was not in love with any boy but her parents forbid her talking to boys and would always reprimand her. She said she was tired of living with her family.

This situation is more or less present, in all households with most parents being scared of their child falling in love and eloping / getting married to someone outside their caste. Love being a universal emotion, all of us have been taught to express love and affection for everyone since childhood. However, the meaning changes when one becomes a teenager and love becomes romance or has sexual connotations. But it is not so and boys and girls can just like each other's company because they can express their thoughts and ideas which are usually accepted by friends unlike parents.

Hence, as a parent if one finds the child staying out late, talking a lot on the phone, being evasive to parents or visiting friends often it is definitely a signal for something happening in their child's life. A parent has to be alert for these signs rather than being a watchdog. Just plain communication with the child, talking as a friend and telling the child the dilemma of the parent would help in resolving many issues.

ii] Prashant was a typical teenager. He liked to go out, visit pubs with his many girlfriends, spend time surfing the net and bunking college. His parents were unaware of his life outside home. They found him to be a well behaved boy who was average in studies. A letter from the college informed them that Prashant had not attended a single lecture and hence he was not eligible to sit for the exams. When they spoke with him, he did not reveal anything. His mother then checked his clothes and cupboard and found some 'bhang (cannabis)' tablets which he was abusing. Many youngsters fall prey to drugs as they like to experience a high with commonly abused drugs like charas or ganja (cannabinoids), brownsugar (opiods) or designer drugs. Many parents are not aware of this fact as there are no telltale signs like in alcohol. Children frequenting pubs, hanging out late with friends are always under peer pressure to try out new things.

Hence, first of all as parents, you have to keep the child under scrutiny, see which pubs he is frequenting, keep an account of all his friends, find out if anything is missing from home or if the child is demanding for more money and of course find out if the child is attending college. More important is to have a heart to heart talk telling the child about your own personal experiences, what things could happen in the college life, so that the child is aware and knows you are there for support. Being dictatorial and stopping pocket money or not allowing the child out of the house would be a solution for few days. We have to look at a permanent solution where the child does not hesitate to tell a friend or a parent if he was done something wrong.

Life is all about making mistakes and learning from them. But don't let the child be lost in his vagrant childhood. Be there, take interest in his activities and communicate to him. Discuss with him, consider him as an adult and give him his responsibilities. Be there to shelter him in crises but don't overprotect him as he will not be able to withstand the challenges in life.

iii] Sometimes as children are pursuing higher studies and want to fulfill parental expectations they may do so, at the cost of their own emotions. Deciding for children is not what we have to do as parents but helping them to decide should be our goal. But many children forsake many of their desires for parental wishes and then they live in a vacuum. They experience no joy in doing those activities or even pursing education. These children become depressed, anxious, and are often worriers. They keep to themselves and their general interest in things reduces. When exams come, they become nervous wrecks, not wanting to appear for exams but on the other hand they also do not want to disappoint their parents. This dilemma continues and we have a child who is irritable, weepy, cranky, not eating or sleeping well and obviously the child is going through a lot of emotional upheaval. When a parent comes across these signs, they should not wait to see a psychiatrist because this situation has come up as the child is disturbed and depressed. Parents have to be alert to their child's eating and sleeping habits as these signs are the first telltale signs of emotional disturbances.

A quiet child should therefore not be left alone but talked to and understood. A referral to a doctor is a must especially if the child expresses no desire to live.

Parenting therefore is the most difficult job. It gives pleasure but the pain is also phenomenal. Being a parent teaches one the art of sacrifice, love, forgiveness and patience. In today's changing world of money, media, machinery parents find it difficult to find time for their grownup teenage children. The mantra is in believing in co-existence, compassion, caring and communication. And yes, if one is able to do all this, majority of the children may not go into these danger zones and even if they do, at least they would come out unscathed.

28 *All In A Smoke*

The joy of entering adolescence brings with it a lot of agony for the parents. The child is now getting prepared to enter adult hood but he already behaves like an adult. "I know what is right for me" "They are my friends", "You just know how to' spoil my mood," "My friends also do it". Well these are some of the issues happening in every household on a daily basis. The phase of 'growing up' gives them a rebellious streak and we often find that children behave differently in their teens. Now they feel very strongly about certain things and hence they voice their opinions. It is only important for then that they should be heard, even if whatever they say may be wrong or impractical.

It so happened that a 15 year old boy got admitted in the hospital on the pretext that his father was threatening to remove him from the house. He was like any other 15 year old. Hair was slightly long and streaked golden at places. The boy came from a typical Maharashtrian middle class background. He admitted that he was consuming "brown sugar"(opiods). He had failed last year in his ninth grade, so his father decided that he should not waste a year again in the ninth but rather appear for his tenth from private classes. So the boy stopped going to school and his father had enrolled him in several classes / tuitions. In the summer holidays the boy had visited his maternal aunt's house in Mumbai where he stayed over for a few days. According to his father, that was the first time they had allowed him to stay over at any relatives house. It so happened that his maternal cousin who was 2 years elder to him introduced him to his group of friends and a substance called "charas" (cannabis).

Now charas or ganja or bhang are all substances that alter the brain and body functioning to such an extent that the person consuming it becomes addicted to the substance. They produce a euphoric effect as a result of which the person feels pleasant and forgets his problems. This boy consumed charas for a few months during which he would often bunk classes and tuitions and started going out with his "new found friends" to a pub called "Madness".

According to him, he was a regular at the discotheque and his friends would end up paying for him. In order to sustain this life style the boy started demanding things at home. He asked for a mobile, a gold chain, which "he then lost" within a few days. As he was taking 'charas' his parents were not able to make out that he was into drugs, though they did get suspicious of his late nights. It so happened that this boy had got so much hooked onto drugs that he had moved on to consuming other substances like "brown sugar" (opiods). In just a span of 1 year, the boy was totally changed in his attitude and behavior. He did not seem to care for self or his family as he continued in this path of high risk behavior.

What one has to understand is that it is not only the children of the rich but all children from any socio-economic strata are extremely vulnerable to develop addiction. Peer pressure is a crucial factor that is responsible for developing addiction. Many boys or girls start experimenting with various drugs like beer, alcohol, charas, sedative drugs, cough syrups, ecstasy etc. in company. The person who does not try is often ridiculed and made to feel left out as a result of which the child gives in to the pressure and then the journey to doom begins. The youngsters have no realization of what 'addiction' entails. They all believe in the misconceptions that "alcohol makes you feel good and bold" or that 'when you take drugs" people feel you're different and look up to you.

As the children start straying away from the families, their communication with their friends' increases but with their families decreases to such an extent, that parents may be completely unaware of what their child is up to. Mobile phones, increased pocket money, pleasure seeking need, different sources of gratification like pubs, food plazas etc. and the ever changing attitude of the society are all a culprit in leading these children to such drug seeking behaviors. Stress, difficulty in coping with studies, over expectation from parents, poor self confidence and low self esteem all add on to provoke the child into experimenting substances to decrease his 'tension'. Children are thus easily influenced by this "escape route" but what they don't realize is the 'chakravyu' that sets in like a vicious cycle from which there is no escape.

What starts as fun may have serious side effects like endangering their lives. The body may protest by manifesting "withdrawal symptoms" like tremors, restlessness, anxiety as in alcohol use disorders but the parents have to be alert to detect these physical and emotional changes that occur. Alcohol use can be made out by the red eyes, smell or the "intoxicated / dazed look". These children often sway and have difficulty in doing routine things properly and there may be heaviness of the tongue and slurring of speech which may be a giveaway sign.

But in order to know if the child is hooked onto charas or brown sugar, there may be some other telltale signs like the child may become restless, may go and lock himself in the room or the bathroom for sometime till he smokes or he may give vague answers about his whereabouts, he may keep late nights or start staying over at friends places or parents may find money or small things like watches, jewellery etc. disappearing from the house.

It is therefore necessary to keep a close watch on the adolescent when he is growing up and there should be a two way communication so that the parent is able to judge what their child's emotional status is.

Seeking help at the right time by taking the child to a psychiatrist or a counselor will help to evaluate the extent of the problem, rather than turning a deaf ear or a blind eye. It is our duty as parents to see that our children's future does not go into smoke!

29 *Exam Phobia*

The worst of the fears come up in children especially during exam time, the most trying of the examinations being the tenth and twelfth. Of course apart from the fact that they are board examinations, they also happen to be the deciding factor of the child's career. The importance given to these exams by the parents and society is enormous leading to increased expectations from the child, who is already surviving under the pressure.

All efforts by parents and teachers are performance oriented, without any parent looking after the emotional needs of the child. The preparation for tenth in some schools begins at least 6 months prior to entering tenth, with the ninth class being taught in a real hurry. The child is enrolled in all possible classes to increase the knowledge. Is this all necessary? I agree there is stiff competition and the child has to pass and score well so that he gets the branch of his choice but is it right to put the child through so much of mental and emotional ordeal?

Somewhere, we as parents have to ask ourselves—how right are we? A child who is intelligent will definitely get marks be it 75% or 80%. His admission to science is guaranteed. Then why is the need that he/she should score above 85% and so on. Colleges everywhere impart the same kind of education. A good college does not necessarily mean good teachers. This is also true of schools. Having children do well academically does tell that the school is very much performance oriented. But it does not say that the school is child friendly. Ultimately we all perform as per our capacity. If we are stretched beyond our coping strategies there are problems. This is seen in the form of numerous emotional and behavioral problems coming up in the children with studies become an ordeal. Even before entering the tenth and twelfth the child is under pressure and tense about his future. Will I pass? Will I get good marks? Will my parents be happy and so on and so forth? These innumerable unanswered questions inhabit his mind which then troubles him. The result being that the once happy child is now worn out, tired, fatigued, complains of headache or multiple pains, lack of concentration difficulty in remembering his studies, loss of appetite and lack of sleep. All these symptoms are of depression which ultimately engulfs the child.

If the parents remain unaware and the child does not let them know in order to ward off their anger, the same child may become suicidal. We are all aware of how impulsive children are and how much scared they are of their tenth and twelfth results. The number of voluntary organizations and help lines that have come up in these last few years is due to the increased stress faced by these children. Somewhere I think we are responsible. The fear of tenth is instilled by us into their minds way before they are in tenth as parents are more worried about their child's performance. The common answer being, if he doesn't study now, how will he do his tenth? The child thus grows up on thinking that tenth is the biggest milestone in his life.

He thus begins to have his own fears about exams which he finds difficult to address. Parents also are in no mood to listen to him. So then what should he do? Well, he tries very hard to cope and when the day arrives of his exams he goes into a state of panic. He breaks into sweat, becomes cold and clammy, his heart races as he thinks the worst moment of his life has come and he trembles and feels that he cannot go and sit for the exams. His entire year of study comes to a standstill for he now refuses to appear for the exams. The parents then go into frenzy as they try to reassure their child. But then aren't we late for that?

All this could have been avoided. The child could have grown on the positive side of exams, where parents could have instilled confidence without repeatedly harboring on tenth and twelfth results. The child would then never fear these exams. What are exams? They are not the ultimate test of intelligence! But most parents forget this and they equate the percentage of marks to being intelligent. When the time comes that you as a parent realize this, you will be proud of your child the way he or she is! We should definitely stimulate the child to produce the best in him but in doing so please remember that he is a human being with limited capacities and emotions. Tampering with the machinery would produce disasters like 'exam phobia' depression and suicide. No parent wants their child to go through this, so be alert and stop demanding. Then, there will be no need to run helter or skelter at the last minute if the child has panicked. But if you feel that your child is definitely finding it stressful to cope, do not hesitate to contact a psychiatrist. Anxiety especially exam phobia is treatable and the anxiety related to exams will be put at rest. The child may require 'anti-anxiety agents' or 'antidepressant medication' to bring back his self esteem and confidence. He can be taught relaxation which will further help him. Depending upon the child's level of stress, he may even require counseling. All this should be done not on eve of the exam but very much will in advance. For the psychiatrist is no God but a mere human. Remember as a parent BE ALERT, BE DE-STRESSED, SO THAT YOUR CHILD IS NOT DISTRESSED!

30 *Career Pressure*

A fifteen years old girl, studying in the tenth grade, a ranker was brought to me by her father after she was shown to 2 neurologists for having persistent headaches. The headaches started 7-8 months ago just after her ninth final exams. She had enrolled herself in classes and the preparation for tenth grade exams were definitely on the way. On speaking to her, she came out as a confident girl who was sure that even though she was having a problem she would secure 85% marks. Her headaches were a daily feature, which were so disabling that over the last 6 months her school attendance has dropped down remarkably.

Her teachers and principal were extremely supportive because she was one of their brilliant students. So even if she didn't give her terminal exams or there was school absenteeism, they were not complaining. Her parents on the other hand also said that they have never pressurized her and they would be happy with whatever she scored. The child herself did not give me any conflicts or overt problems with school, family or friends.

She was a typically studious, well adjusted girl who suddenly had found herself incapacitated with her headaches. She had gone to doctors who were headache specialists but there was no improvement. The improvement was not seen because her `headaches' were a symptom of the stress which she was facing and which has to be handled.

Being an extremely confident and bright child she did not worry about passing or doing well and she did ensure that despite not studying regularly she could still cope and take up, the science stream, for she dreamt of becoming a doctor. Everything was fine and she was pursuing her dreams like thousands of others. But then somewhere along the line, I believe her own expectations of herself gave her the blow. Tenth and twelfth grades in our country are the extremely trying years for the youngsters who may then buckle under the pressure.

Continuous studying, multiple classes and no relaxation are extremely taxing. The end result being that the confident child becomes cranky, nervous, jittery and confused about giving exams. If this is what happens to intelligent children, imagine what would be the plight of the mediocre children. Then start the complaints of stomachaches, acidity, vomiting, tension, panic, headaches, giddiness etc . . . . There is just no end to it. Many of the children may also be depressed and may feel that they would never pass and that it would be better if they were dead. Thus depression is a very serious thing to deal with as it emotionally cripples the normal child and takes away the smile from his face.

The child himself is confused about what to do in life. Many parents may not even discuss beyond science, arts and commerce. So the child is in a dilemma. For him a career can be made if one opts for only these 3 streams. Of course, times have changed and a drastic change has come in the people's outlook regarding career choices. The media has been instrumental in reaching out to the masses and spreading awareness about options that are unimaginable and easily attainable. Yes you can make a profession of being a DJ, VJ or RJ and feel proud about it. Today being a doctor or engineer is not the only answer. So though things are changing for the better in the world, the change has to still happen in our homes.

The parent should be there to tell the child about the various options and if need be go to career guidance centers themselves to understand the options. Each parent should be aware of their child's areas of interests, likes, dislikes and their child's inclination towards studies. These should be discussed with the child not after the tenth results but prior to going to tenth grade so that the child is clear about issues and is not under pressure to perform. He should be allowed to reach out to the stars as is his potential with the parent being the 'guiding star'. It should not be parental wishes that are ladled on to the child who takes up science because his father wants him to be a doctor. The world is a huge place and yes every profession survives. What are needed are the right ingredients of zeal, commitment and desires to dish up the right recipe of the perfect career choice.

Your child can avail of the aptitude tests to know which field his inclination lies and there are career counselors who can help. Remember sometimes there may be no 'pressure' from the parents to perform and produce results and parents feel assured that they have not mentally tortured their child. But then, they have not done their duty in understanding or alleviating the "internal pressures" of their child which has resulted in the problem.

What we can give our children is time, help and experience. We may not be extremely knowledgeable, so we accept our limitations. But we should not prevent our child from exploring his potentials. For if the world would only be full of doctors and engineers there would be crises— so we need artists, painters, entertainers and all others to look after the needs of society where every individual has a responsibility and a role to play. Therefore be a 'mentor' to your child and not a 'dictator' when deciding career options.